NO ONE SHALL CALL
ME HOME

"America's New Orphans"

by Rev. James J. Close

TABLE OF CONTENTS

DEDICATION

To my Mom and Dad and to all who have walked at my side in caring for homeless kids, to the faithful donors who continue to contribute so that we have a home to call these kids to, and especially to the boys and girls who make their home with me.

With heartfelt thanks, I dedicate these pages.

Fr. Jim Close

Rev. James J. Close
Superintendent

"There are only two lasting bequests we can give our children, one is roots, the other wings."

INTRODUCTION

"What does a priest know about raising kids?"
People sometimes ask me that.
"Not much," I usually answer.

Because, let's face it—raising kids, especially teen-agers, is a challenging job and an inexact science.

I say that in all sincerity and with a deep sense of humility, despite the fact that I have been unofficial "father" to hundreds of teenage boys and girls during my seventeen years as Superintendent of Mercy Boys' Home in Chicago.

More often than not, my greatest successes with troubled kids have been the result of the trial-and-error method of child raising. And sometimes it's only after many trials and errors that a kid and I really begin to communicate and understand one another.

Now I realize that the kids who come to our Home aren't your typical teens in many ways. Most have grown up not in one, but many, difficult home situations. And my boys and girls come not with one, but

3

many, complex problems.

And I am fortunate to have a staff of dedicated professionals to help me. In addition to offering suggestions, they perform the invaluable service of keeping me on track when I grow weary. Being on one's toes all the time does take its toll.

But as it's often been said, experience is the best teacher. So, rather than thinking of this book as a "how-to" guide on raising kids, I'd like you to think of the stories I've included as my way of sharing what I have learned about kids through my work. I am greatly concerned about America's kids and want to share my solicitude with you.

Perhaps you, or someone you know, is having some special difficulty with a child. Or perhaps your children are still young, and you want to know more about what you can do now to help ward off problems that may lie ahead. Or perhaps — and I hope this is true for you—you are concerned about kids and would just like to know more about the kids who come to our Home.

Most likely, you will never meet the boys and girls to whom I'm going to introduce you, but you may meet someone like them. And when you do, I hope that my words come back to you as a source of strength and direction.

The Mercy kids are some of the most courageous and extraordinary persons I have ever met. Many have overcome immense odds to succeed in life. Others were not so fortunate. But each of them taught me about life and made me grateful for the simple blessings to be found in each day. The stories I share with you include the most important lessons I have learned in my many years of working with kids.

To protect the kids and their families, I have changed names and identifying aspects in their stories. You will note that I've divided the book into two main sections—ROOTS and WINGS.

In the ROOTS section, I will introduce you to a few of the thousands of kids who have at one point in their lives been part of our Mercy Home family. Through their stories, I hope to acquaint you with both the kinds of kids who come to our doors for help and the many problems they bring with them.

The WINGS section highlights, again through our kids' own stories and examples, the successes and failures of our work.

In the EPILOGUE, I want to share with you my personal reflections—"a Close look," if you will—on my years of work with troubled teenagers and on how and why these kids keep coming to Mercy Boys' Home. In addition to giving you more detailed information about our programs, I have included my opinions as to why so many more kids seem to need help today.

These "new orphans," as I prefer to call them, represent an ever growing number of boys and girls. Their lives are so complicated and out of control at an early age that they are literally "throwaway" kids whom their families reject and nobody else wants.

And, just in case you are one of these kids, or a parent of such a kid, and recognize that you need help, I have included our address along with some nationwide "hotlines" to put you in touch with people who can help you.

Because of the prayers and financial support of our friends, our Home has been able to keep its doors open to troubled girls and boys for over a hundred years.

I want to salute these friends, for it is only with their interest and financial support that our work with kids, America's future, has continued through the years and can continue in the years ahead.

As I write, I think of the members of my staff who have given me their friendship, advice, and patient support during my years here. I have good reason to be grateful.

I send a special note of thanks to Jacqueline Lowery Corn for her help in the final writing and editing of this book.

Most of all, I want to thank the kids who have come and continue to come to our doors for help. They have touched and enriched my life and the lives of those who have worked on their behalf in a most special way.

Each boy and girl remains with me—and all of us—in love and spirit. May they and all who find a bit of themselves in these pages have the two greatest legacies that I, as a concerned "Father" can give— ROOTS and WINGS.

God bless you!

Rev. James J. Close

ROOTS

"Can a mother forget her infant,
   be without tenderness for the child
      of her womb?
Even should she forget,
   I will never forget you.
See, upon the palms of my hands
   I have written your name ..."

Isaiah 49:15-16*

Chapter One

NO ONE TO CALL
ME HOME

Johnny read about my work at Mercy Boys' Home in a newspaper article. He called and asked if I would visit him. His place of residence was the Cook County Jail. He was awaiting trial for armed robbery.

I had a few years of experience at the Home by this time, and, I have to admit, I was a bit suspicious of his motives. After all, I didn't even know him. But I went.

I saw the kind of kid I expected to see. Nineteen, thin, and worn looking — with sad, dark eyes that had seen too much of the seamy side of life for too long.

"Thanks for coming, Father," he said. "I—uh, wanted to talk to you."

I nodded.

He told me about when he was a little kid, maybe six or seven. His dad was mean and hit him around a lot. There was always fighting and yelling. His mom didn't pay much attention to anything. She was the only one working. And she was tired most of the time.

He liked it a lot when the weather got warm and he could play outside in the street with the rest of the kids

8

in the neighborhood.

"Our street was as big as the universe to me then," he said, smiling a little.

"When it started getting dark, the other kids' moms would lean out the windows and start calling to their kids, 'Billy, Joey,—it's time to come home.'

"I'd stay out there and keep playing until I was alone. I was always the last one to go home."

"I always had to decide when to go in. There was never anyone to call me in—to call me home."

What do you say to a kid like Johnny ... now thirteen or fourteen years too late? I still felt new at working with troubled kids, and I didn't know anything to say to him, so I just sat there.

"I think sometimes ... that maybe if there were somebody ... just sometime ... I wouldn't be here," he added. "I just wanted to tell you that."

He was very choked up by this time, and he looked away so I wouldn't see the tears welling up in his eyes.

He looked very young to be in so much trouble.

He had a history of run-ins with the law since his early teens, so there wasn't much hope that the system was going to waste any more time with him. He would be in prison a long while. And from there, when he did get out, things didn't look especially promising either. There was no one on the outside who cared about him or who would take him in.

There was still *no one to call him home*.

We finished our visit and went on with our lives. I never heard from Johnny again. But his words haunt me to this day.

Like Johnny, I also grew up in one of Chicago's less affluent neighborhoods. My Mom and Dad were first generation Irish immigrants, the only members of their families to come to the United States.

We were poor, like most of the folks in my neighborhood. Life was pretty much a hand-to-mouth existence. There were eventually six of us kids—four boys and two girls.

We didn't have a lot of material things, and we didn't have any relatives to befriend us or help us out.

We happened to be Irish, but my family could just as easily have been Hispanic, Afro-American, German, Polish, Chinese, Vietnamese, Native American, or one of the hundreds of other ethnic groups who are part of the "all-American" community that makes up our society.

You don't have to pin our troubles on our ethnic, or minority backgrounds. Cities and towns throughout the United States are teeming with thousands of families who have been here for many generations, and who find themselves just as alone in their struggles.

Back then, what most of us shared was our poverty. But I suspect few of us ever thought we were "poor". Today, what all of us share is our isolation from one another. There seems to be so many divisions to keep people apart. And yet, what all of us hope for is a better life.

I was one of the lucky ones, because my family had something going for it that a lot of today's families don't seem to have. We had each other, and we had a Mom and Dad to care about us.

We had a home where all of us were wanted and loved.

Yet, that wasn't enough to qualify me to be in charge of Mercy Boys' Home, and I knew it.

So, back in 1973, when I was told to go to there, I wasn't too happy about it at first.

Father Ed Kelly, who had headed the Home for thirty-nine years, was a living legend in the city of Chicago. His was a hard act to follow, and his job was a difficult one. Besides, I reasoned, what did I know about kids, especially kids with problems.

The first ten years after my ordination, I had spent in an outstanding, blue-collar parish with large, happy, hard-working families. I, too, had worked hard getting a sports program going for the kids in addition to my other duties. I loved the parishioners. I felt I had earned their respect and friendship. I liked where I was a lot.

But Father Kelly had suffered a stroke and needed help. I was "volunteered". That's the way it was back then. When you were told to do something, you obeyed. No questions asked. That was your commitment.

Unfortunately, Father Kelly was also gravely ill with cancer and died within six months after my arrival at the Home. I was appointed the new Superintendent.

I was very green and very naive. I made many mistakes, some of them several times. Then I made the right mistakes for the wrong reasons. After the first few months of struggling, I was ready to give up.

The problems of the kids I saw were overwhelming.

Our finances and resources were always strained.

Mercy Boys' Home was a large, rambling red brick structure built back around 1910 or before. It had long, dark halls and institution-like dorms with rows of beds—real Orphan Annie stuff.

Things broke and had to be fixed. There were reports to do, bills to be paid, funds to raise from somewhere, somehow, and a mountain of details to tackle. Most importantly, however, the needs of the kids were great, and more than I felt I could handle.

I wasn't even sure I was cut out to be a "father" to unwanted and hurting teenagers who had been booted in and out of dozens of homes most of their lives.

I guess the only thing I did have going for me was that I cared about those kids.

I wanted, above all else, to make a home for them where they would be fed, clothed, and sheltered—a home where they would feel safe, loved, and cared about—a home where they could grow, change, and put their lives back together.

What I wanted, I realized, was a miracle that would re-occur a thousand times over. I wanted a miracle for every kid who knocked on our door.

Yet I couldn't stop thinking that if I could somehow create a home atmosphere where our kids really felt loved, missed, and a part of our Mercy family, I would have done a lot.

After all, that is the most basic part of "parenting" is it not—creating a home and a loving family?

So this became my first goal.

I wanted to make sure—that at least at Mercy Boys'

Home — there would always be someone to call the kids home—kids like Johnny.

Chapter Two

YOU'RE PUTTING ME ON

One of the most striking things about many of the kids who come to Mercy Boys' Home is that they don't know they're different from anybody else.

They may have been raised in the most bizarre and disfunctional family situation imaginable. But they don't know that. Unlike the middle class kids with whom most of us are more familiar—the kids who often gripe because they don't have all the clothes, toys, and things which their friends have—the majority of my kids don't know what they are missing, at least at first they don't.

This fact has been brought home to me again and again, but perhaps never so powerfully as when we take a kid who comes to us from a more "normal" family. Bruce was one of these kids.

Shortly after he arrived, I took him down to the dining room where the rest of the boys were eating supper. Because a new kid sometimes stirs the waters by promoting a fight as a way to establish himself with the group, I usually stay within earshot for the first day or so, but enough out of the way so that conversation can still flow freely among the boys.

As I suspected, before long, Bruce was trying to impress his peers by telling them about a trip he had taken with his mom and dad to a theme park the previous summer.

The boys at the table listened to him in utter amazement, looking perplexed and downright disbelieving.

"Oh, right, sure!" Tony finally said, rather sarcastically.

Bruce ignored the "put-down" and continued his glowing report of rides and souvenirs.

Tony's challenge got a bit more forceful and to the point. "I don't believe you."

"There's no way you could've seen both of your parents at the same time," chimed in one of the other boys at the table.

Now it was Bruce's turn to look confused.

The conversation opened up to the entire group. The consensus was that Bruce was lying. None of the boys thought it was possible to be with both parents at the same time.

Most of them had never even seen their fathers. A few had been abandoned by their mothers as well. Their typical experience so often was—living with a grandmother or another relative, then on to a series of foster homes. Mom drifted in and out of their lives. Occasionally "brothers" and "sisters" drifted in as well. They came to live with them for a few months or a year—usually shortly after mom remarried or started living with a new "dad". This living arrangement, too, was short-lived, just like the many others.

The new "dad" eventually had it and left. The mom often got frustrated and moved out. It was back to being bounced around between relatives and foster homes. So/the beat went on ... until Mercy Boys' Home took them in.

The most frightening thing about the situation I've related is that such situations are all too common among kids at Mercy Boys' Home. Our kids have so few of the simple family experiences that most kids have growing up, it nearly boggles the mind.

I'm not talking here about ritzy family vacations and Christmas Eve around the fireplace. I'm talking about food in the refrigerator, and the same bed every night.

The teenager in our Home was probably born into an addicted family. His or her mother abused drugs and alcohol throughout pregnancy, and received little, if any, medical care.

The infant had many after effects from this prenatal abuse, and may even have been born addicted or with a debilitating disease or with one or more disabilities.

Mom and dad, if dad were around at all, may have been drug dealers and users. They seldom married one another.

While scarcely more than a youngster, our kids may have started experimenting with drugs or joined a gang. In fact, some of our kids asked to come to live with us because they were next on the list to be killed.

Any number of our kids have been rejected and disowned by both parents. Many have been abandoned by foster or adoptive parents as well. They have been abused physically, psychologically, and sexually from an early age. Some have been prostitutes, at times even pushed into this way of life by their own parents.

They have lived in ten to twelve or more homes and failed in every school they attended. Most have numerous learning disabilities and are several years below grade level in reading and other academic skills.

Because of their history of failure and deprivation, they have no sense of identity, and feel depressed, hopeless, and absolutely alone in life. Any number are suicidal.

A vacation with two parents to a theme park? Hey, really!

After being around our kids and wallowing around in their histories for so many years, I myself sometimes have a hard time remembering there are such things as "normal" families.

Knowing what our kids have come from and the way they have lived only serves to make me more aware of how far we have to travel with them. Just to bring them back and give them even a few of the experiences they have missed is a monumentally expensive effort, plus a huge human investment from my staff.

Will they make it, even if we try?

Will the love and caring we give them at Mercy Boys' Home be enough to undo even a fraction of the misery they have suffered?

Will they ever be able to give more than they had to their own kids someday, or will they perpetuate their cycle of poverty, misery, addiction, and abuse?

Is it too late for them? Will they make it as adults?

Thoughts like these often run through my mind. I get rid of them quickly. Maybe because I'm a born optimist, but mostly because I really believe things can be different for our kids.

Fortunately, after seventeen years, I have enough success stories to keep me going. This is my life's work. Luckily, my fellow workers share this commitment.

At Mercy Boys' Home, we've bought into the hope that we can help these "new orphans" and throwaway kids who have landed upon our doorsteps.

The best news is that we are making good things happen for these kids, and these kids are making good things happen for themselves.

So, as long as there are kids who need our help, we'll be here for them. And as long as these kids keep believing that things can be different for them and that they can know some of the joy, happiness, and success which have eluded them this far—we'll keep trying harder to do more for them.

We're into our second century of taking care of kids. In what I've learned of family life so far, Mercy Boys' Home will be a haven for kids in need even when our third century of service begins. When we're gone, we'll see to it that there will be someone else to continue our work.

Because, the way I see it, where there is life, there is always the possibility for change and growth. I'm not going to "throw away" any kid before he or she has at least been given a chance to make it.

Chapter Three

BUYING IN

I broke my own rules and took in Mike at age 13. Our program is most effective for children who are at least fourteen years old. In Mike's case I made an exception. For a long while, it looked as if I were going to live to regret it.

Mike was a constant truant, and a constant source of trouble to his "family" — an unemployed, alcoholic mother who didn't know where she was most of the time, much less Mike.

Mike had virtually no supervision at home and kept himself from going hungry by hustling newspapers or earning a few dollars in whatever way he could. A 3 year-old shouldn't have to support himself.

He was so young and innocent looking. I started out with visions of grandeur of what might be possible for him once he had food, clothing, and shelter he could count on. I even squeezed in a haircut. After all, despite the fact that he had been on his own for most of his life, he was basically a good kid and had never gotten into serious trouble.

Anyway, like most of our kids, Mike was several years behind in school. Why shouldn't he be? He never went. He was out working to survive.

I put Mike in a special school where he could get the

special attention and tutoring he needed to catch up.

The problem was, he never went to that school either.

For the sixty boys living at Mercy Boys' Home at any one time, we utilize the services of some twenty-five Catholic, public, and private schools, vocational programs, alternative education programs, and G.E.D. programs.

The reason for this is that we attempt to match up a kid with an educational program that best meets his needs and in which he can succeed. We do the same for the girls at Mercy Girls' Home.

So, every morning our kids head off to school on buses and trains, or by car or on foot, to get to school—just like most families in America do each day.

Well, Mike seldom got there.

Like the rest of the kids, he'd dutifully take his bus fare, books, and lunch and leave at the appointed time. Then, as soon as he was out my sight, he'd head off for God knows where to spend the day.

Since we have a close working relationship with our kids' schools and communicate with their teachers daily, we'd get a call from his principal when he wasn't there.

Life was becoming a series of daily hassles that threatened my sanity and peaked one day when the police escorted Mike home.

If ever I experienced what it must be like to be a parent and know a feeling of total failure and disappointment in your child, this was the day. Mike, I was politely informed, has been picked up at Union Station for stealing a woman's purse.

Fortunately, the woman and the police were content to see that Mike was simply back in our care. So, once the police left, I lit into Mike with a lecture you wouldn't believe.

Stealing was wrong. School was right. Education was the only way to improve yourself and your chances of getting a good job someday. What would it be like if we all stole from one another? What would Mercy Boys' Home be like if we didn't respect one another's property? Stealing was dishonest . . . I was even leading up to what I thought was the clincher—the Ten Commandments and sin.

Like I've said before, I was very naive in my early days here.

Mike offered no defense. Instead, as I talked, his face grew more and more perplexed, and his eyes widened. Before long, I realized we had a communication problem. So I shut up, which is what I probably should have done in the first place.

Mike told his side as I listened.

"It was true," he said. He stole the lady's purse.

"But," he said, somewhat proudly, "this is the first time I ever got caught."

He was sorry that he had gotten caught and sorry for all the trouble he had caused me.

Then his story unfolded . . . He had been stealing purses since he was ten. He started on this way of life after he and a neighborhood kid rolled a drunk and netted enough cash for each of them to buy a new pair of gym shoes. These were the first pair of new shoes Mike had ever had.

He began an occasional stake-out at Union Station. He watched the travelers and picked out his victims— almost always women. He was very proud of the fact that he never hurt any of them.

"I always had money before I came here," he bragged.

I asked him about his victims. Didn't they have rights? Didn't they have a right to their own money? He had an answer for that, too.

"If they travel, they must be rich," he declared.

Clearly, crime did pay for Mike. And clearly, he figured it was okay. School and education were far-off goals that didn't impact his life very much at the present time.

The good thing was that Mike already "kind of liked it" with us. He had started buying into things like security, love, trust, and concern for others. But he just wasn't quite there yet.

It took some months, but he began to like school. He also began to like us even more. With just a few peaks and valleys, Mike went on to graduate from high school and then college. And, as far as I know, he has chosen the straight and narrow path.

Kids like Mike, who are deprived of material things, present a special challenge to us.

Getting them to see that there is a better way than stealing or hustling drugs, even if it might not pay off as quickly, is difficult. Our kids tend to have a low level of tolerance for frustration and waiting.

They act quickly, impulsively, and most of the

time, without thinking of the consequences of their actions. Much of the time, it pays off for them, despite the fact that someone innocent might be victimized in the process.

Our biggest problem with kids like this is a marketing one. We have to convince them to "buy into" our program. Before accepting them, they have to want help, but sometimes just wanting help is not enough. It's too long to wait. Dirty dollars bring immediate results.

Although our kids have freedom, there are also restrictions. Once they come to live in our family, they must go to school or be involved in some type of educational program. They must have a job if they are able to work. They must attend group counseling sessions with the other kids and staff members at the Home. Many times, more extensive private therapy is needed as well. And underlying it all, they must recognize the need for changes in their behavior and attitudes and be willing to work on growing up to be conscientious citizens.

Then, there are the "nuts and bolts" of our program. They must adjust to being members of our family.

Eating meals at set times in the dining room, instead of fast food in front of the TV.

Sharing recreational facilities, the telephone, and the television.

Not using drugs or alcohol.

Keeping curfew hours.

Not "borrowing" another's property without asking permission.

Working to earn privileges and weekend passes, and losing them when they fail to comply with the program.

It's a whole lot to ask, especially with kids who have had only erratic discipline and nurturing. But it's the only way we can operate. Without structure and set expectations, our Home would be in constant chaos.

By the time they come to live with us, our kids have a clear idea of what will be expected of them. But, kids being kids, some of it they resist.

On the bright side, they know they will be taken care of in a safe, secure, and caring environment. They will have consistent, supportive, and trusting relationships they can count on. They will have opportunities to grow and develop as persons, as future workers, and as citizens.

Most of our kids want all these things. But we still have to sell them on our program to get them where they want to go.

When I get discouraged, I have only to talk to "regular" parents, most of whom have a hard time making their own kids buy into the values they have been trying to instill since birth.

Having a kid since birth is a distinct advantage. But a boy or girl comes into our world when they are somewhere between being a child and an adult. Our kids come with pre-set ideas, often of questionable value, and many times with a lack of self-discipline.

Statistically, about ninety-five percent of kids do eventually buy into the things their parents preached.

If the parents have been consistent with discipline and have modeled the behaviors they desire in their kids, the odds are great that their kids will turn out according to parental expectations as adults.

At Mercy Boys' Home, our success rate isn't always that high, but we never give up trying.

We have kids who are simply too bruised, beat up and bent emotionally to trust us, or anyone else. They have a hard time accepting our values and a harder time believing in our program.

Over the years, I have come at least to understand why. If all you've known is disappointment, if all you've been told is what a loser you are, if all you've seen is poverty and life on the other side of the law—it is hard to believe things can ever change for someone like you.

We work to convince these kids it is worthwhile to change. We try hard to communicate this to our kids and, through our prevention programs, to other kids in the community who aren't in such bad shape yet.

Although we can't give every kid a whole new deck of cards with which to play the game of life, I like to think that Mercy Boys' Home can reshuffle the hand they've been dealt and perhaps add a few cards of our own to help these boys and girls come out on top for a change.

Chapter Four

BACK TO BASICS

Everyone knew her as the "Burger King" girl. But Barbara's nickname really had nothing to do with food. The fast-food shop was where she hung out, day and night—whenever she could keep two steps ahead of the school authorities and the police.

Not that the police ever have much time to hassle kids like Barbara. With Chicago's long list of "serious crime", the police stay mighty busy without worrying about curfew violations and loitering.

She was an extraordinarily pretty girl, with a fresh, girl-next-door look that belied her years on the streets. She was only 14, but quickly going on 19.

It all happened some years back. Fortunately, it was at a time when I had a place for her to go.

Ever since I came to Mercy Boys' Home, I dreamed of opening a home for girls. Often entire families would be referred to us. We'd take the boys in, but had to say no to the girls because of the physical limitations of our Home. When this happened, the brothers and sisters from one family often didn't have a lot of contact with one another. I knew this separation was not in their best interest. Considering the difficult childhood most had, they very much needed the support of one another.

From my personal life I know first-hand the value of brotherly and sisterly love. So, from the beginning, I set about opening a Mercy Girls' Home.

My first attempt in the mid-70s failed after a short while, not because of our program, but surprisingly for me because of a lack of referrals for girls who needed long-term, residential care. I might add, before I get on with Barbara's story, that we have had no problem filling Mercy Girls' Home again in the summer of 1988. Maybe that in itself says something about the state of kids in our society today.

In my early experience the basic reason for the shortage of girls needing this kind of home was that so often some relative would come forward to take the girl in. Somehow, admitting they had a "problem" girl was more than they wanted to own up to. The boys were easier to part with because everyone knew boys will be boys.

I guess it's still part of the infamous double standard, but with a different twist. It's bad to have failed with a boy, but to have failed with a girl attaches an additional social stigma. There is a deeper wound to it and the problems are more complex, as any parent with a troubled young lady can attest.

Then there's that old myth. Girls are easier to raise. I don't know who started that one, but most of the professionals in my business haven't found that to be the case, not the kind of girls referred to us anyway.

At the time Barbara's case came to my attention, we had just opened our first Mercy Girls' Home in the old, closed down Angel Guardian Orphanage—a true "sister" building to Mercy Boys' Home in age and style.

Once she got used to the idea of having someone around to help her, Barbara thought she was in heaven. She loved it. It was the first time in her life that she had her very own bed, a nightstand, clothes, and meals she could rely on.

"Every day's like Christmas here," she told me excitedly.

Let me tell you, it's compliments like that that "make my day," especially when they come from kids like Barbara, who had such deep hurts to heal. It's amazing she would still gamble on reaching out to anyone at all.

Shortly after her arrival, I was visiting the girls and thought I'd take them on a guided tour and point out some of the building's qualities.

We got to the chapel. At either side of the double doors were two enormous—and I mean life-size enormous—guardian angel holy water fonts. They were made out of some kind of white polished stone or marble. Together, they were a most impressive sight, standing watch over God's house like winged sentinels.

Barbara, who was not Catholic, studied the angels a long while.

"I'm not going in there," she said emphatically.

Later, when walking alone with her, I asked her why she wouldn't go into the chapel.

"I don't talk to God anymore 'cuz he never listens to me."

I was taken aback by the matter of fact tone of her words. But, more than that, I was saddened. I envi-

sioned Barbara as a little girl again, back in the days
when maybe her mom wasn't in as bad a shape as she
now was, when maybe Barbara's life had some sem-
blance of security and happiness.

Like most mothers, Barbara's mom probably told
her about God and prayed with her. Or maybe she
just took Barbara to Sunday School and somebody
taught her there.

Like most kids, Barbara probably wanted to believe
that God loved her and listened to her prayers.

So she prayed, but her mom still kept drinking and
began getting more abusive and psychotic.

"Help me brush these needles out of my hair,
Barbara. Our neighbors don't like us, and they're
trying to kill me," her mom would tell her.

She'd have to stand for hours brushing her mom's
hair. There would be nothing there she could see, but
she played along and brushed and brushed to keep her
mom happy.

The man she knew as "dad," who was really not
related at all, deserted them as her mother's paranoia
grew worse. Lots of men followed in her mother's life.

Barbara would come home from school and find
them in bed together. Invited to join them at times,
she'd run out of their house.

Then her grandmother died. She couldn't go there
anymore when she needed a place to hide.

They were always between apartments it seemed. She
had been in so many different schools that she couldn't
even remember them all. And she had no time to make
friends. Just about the time she'd meet someone who

could overlook her dirty, raggy clothes and stringy hair and want to be her friend, her mother would be behind in the rent and they had to move again.

"You look a mess," one of her classmates told her on picture day. And a few of her teachers were no better.

"Surely, your mother can wash your clothes and cut your hair," Miss Adams told her sharply in second grade. "You're probably infecting this entire class with lice."

And somewhere along the line, during all this, Barbara stopped praying. At the old age of eight or nine, she had lost faith in herself, her mom, and God.

Here I was, someone she had known only a few days, trying to nudge her into a church, a family, and a lifestyle she had never experienced. She later told me that because of her refusal to go into the chapel, she thought I'd get rid of her.

"You won't let me stay here very long. I know you won't," she said.

After all, that's how it always ended for her, wasn't it?

I tried to convince her that God and lots of other people were still on her side, and that she could stay with us as long as she wanted to. It was a lot to accept, for Barbara or for any other kid coming from her life experiences.

That day Barbara got me to wondering. What was it that wounded her the most? Was it the fact that the basics—food, clothing, shelter—had been so hard to come by? Was it her severely disturbed mother? Or was it that her dreams and her faith had failed her?

I've seen kids go through a lot with just their faith and their dreams holding them together. Sometimes, those are the deciding factors about who survives at all.

That's one of the reasons we encourage our kids to give God and faith a second chance.

It's difficult at first, getting our kids to church, and many of them just go through the motions of going. They can attend the church of their choice, and we encourage them to go. They can gripe before and after and often do—but they are expected to go.

Over their months and years with us, I usually see lots of good changes in them. I can't say it's all because we got a kid believing in God again. But then I can't say it's only because of what we did for them either.

I'm a strong believer in the power of prayer combined with effort and love. Those things, taken together, are some solid basics for our kids to latch onto. I like to see that each of our kids tries things with God on their side.

Chapter Five

I'VE COME TO LIVE HERE

The doorbell rang one cold winter night. It was about 9 p.m., and I was a bit apprehensive about answering it.

Mercy Boys' Home is not in a residential part of town. We're just out of the downtown area, and there are few homes in the area.

Then, too, we have an ample share of Chicago's homeless drifting up and down our street. They see the sign "MISSION OF OUR LADY OF MERCY" on the front of the building and assume they have found a shelter for the night.

Expecting to see someone looking for a bed or a handout, I opened the door. Standing before me was a scruffy looking kid, about 15 years old, his shoulders scrunched under his thin jacket, his hands and head bare. His thin face broke into a million-dollar smile.

"Hi," he said. "My name's Danny Macclossen. I've come to live here."

Our admission procedure is usually a bit more formal than that, but I let him in out of the cold. I'm a soft touch for a gutsy kid. I told him it was because my name was Close, which is a lot like Macclossen, and maybe we were related.

My joking to the contrary, I knew I had to do some

calling if he was even going to spend the night. We don't take in runaways generally. Runaways usually have parents who are worried sick about them. And most of these runaway kids return home after just a few days or weeks on the streets.

Before I could get into a discussion about the legality of his being there however, Danny hinted I offer him something to eat, preferably something warm.

"It's been a long time since I ate," he said in a hopeful tone, his face lighting up again with that charismatic smile. He had been staying at a shelter for alcoholics the past day or so. One of the men there finally sobered up enough to realize Danny was just a kid and in the wrong place.

"You need to go over a couple blocks to Mercy Boys' Home," the guy told Danny. "The priest will take you in."

Danny told me he had ridden the rails all the way from the state of Washington, made it all the way without one cent.

As I was heating up some soup for him in the kitchen, I dropped the bomb on him.

"You can spend the night, or maybe even stay. But you have to call your mom and let her know that you're here,"I said.

"No way," he said adamantly and turned to leave.

He gave the heating soup a last wistful glance. Then his hunger or his memories of the cold got the better of him. He slowed his pace towards the door.

"Maybe we can talk about it," he said.

"Maybe you can call," I said. "Now."

His mom was happy to hear from him, but didn't seem particularly worried about him. He was the fourth of her five kids to run away. She didn't know where any of the others were either.

"He was probably right to run away," she told me.

Danny's father was a violent, abusive alcoholic. The family situation was flagrantly disordered, and there wasn't anything for Danny to go back to. Some kids do have good reason for running away!

We worked things out so that he could stay, and I showed him to his bedroom. Another arrival with only the shirt on his back. It wasn't until a couple of days later that Danny realized we were a Catholic sponsored Home.

My assurances that we took in kids in need and didn't look at baptismal records did little to assuage his feelings of anxiety. Finally, he blurted out that he had been raised hearing a lot of bad stories about Catholics.

He remained leery of us. But his immediate needs for food and shelter outweighed his uneasiness about us. Besides, I had thrown in a new pair of jeans and a warmer jacket.

It didn't take Danny long to learn the ropes. He was one of those rare, optimistic kids who doesn't easily get beaten down by life. You know the saying, "When life hands you lemons, make lemonade"? Danny was the kind of kid who turned them into lemon meringue pie.

Within a week, he had himself enrolled in one of the most elite private schools in Chicago. He had pretended that he was from a wealthy family and gave an address on Lake Shore Drive. That's quite a "hustle" for a kid of barely fifteen years. I had to smile to myself.

I emphatically informed him he had to tell the truth. Reluctantly he did, and miraculously the school kept him plus reducing his tuition considering we had to pick up the bill.

In my book, Danny already had his degree as a master "con artist."

Right then, I knew that he had what it takes to go all the way to the top if he could just get a little love and support.

Our second mutual crisis came when he found out he had to go to church on Sundays. He wasn't fond of Catholics. But he was also turned off by the religious faith he was raised in, too.

Since the Catholics at Mercy Boys' Home, in Danny's opinion, had it "easier" because I said Mass for them in our chapel, he agreed he would "sit in" on "the services". I presume he thought I wouldn't notice if he were there or not.

He was wrong.

For the next five or six months, Danny attended Mass on Sundays. He sat in the last pew with his arms crossed in front of him and stared at the ceiling or the floor. Over the couple of years he lived with us, he began moving up, pew by pew.

By the time he left us—he had won a full scholarship to the University of Chicago—he was near the front of the chapel and actually paying attention and singing along with us.

As an added note of interest, before I get into some of the things I learned from Danny about life, I might mention that during the summer of his Junior year, he went to Ireland and looked up my relatives, whom I'd never known, seen, or heard from. He confused them thoroughly by introducing himself as "one of my kids," after telling them I was a priest.

Not all of "my" kids have the personality and determination of Danny. Adversity, poverty, and lack of love seem to have one of two effects on the kids we see.

Either, like Danny, with a little help, they defy all odds and overcome their circumstances. Or like a lot of the kids I see, they give up early and begin dying the slow death that most keep as a lifetime companion.

It's not that the latter type doesn't want to succeed. They just have a hard time believing they are worth the effort. They see themselves as having something wrong with them, resigned to a life of failure and trouble, often just like their families. Drugs, alcohol, sex, and violence are a few of the ways they anesthesize the pain of this slow suicide.

Most of them don't talk about it, but when you get them in the right mood — after they trust you enough—they might say something like, "Well, I'm pretty dumb," or "Nothing good's ever going to happen to me—that's the way I am".

Then, most often, they set out to make their prophesies come true—by quitting jobs or getting themselves fired, by running away and moving around a lot, by abusing drugs and alcohol, or by joining gangs in a last-ditch effort to be somebody before the nobody they expect to be moves in permanently. After they've lost enough battles, losing the war is easy.

Do I succeed with all these kids?

No, I don't. But even the kids whom I judged to be on a dead end street, do change for the better. Maybe a few months or years down the road, a little splinter of what I try to instill in them begins to motivate them to do something about the chronic pain and desperation they live with.

Slowly, they begin to make a few changes. And, like Danny's experience with church, it's moving up little by little that gets them to the front.

In my business, you can't look for success in prestige, bonuses, or company perks. Sometimes, all it takes are the words, "I want things to be different for me" and a smile from a scruffy kid.

Chapter Six

A FAMILY AFFAIR

Good things come in bunches. So do troubles and kids sometimes.

The Garcia family got to be such a big bunch, I wasn't sure Mercy Boys' Home would ever see the end of them.

It began routinely enough when the police found Jose and his two younger brothers sleeping in a car. Sensing that there was more to this than a few runaways, the police brought them to me. They thought they were rescuing the boys from a recent family problem that had put the kids out on the street.

What they didn't know was that the kids had been sleeping in cars off and on the better part of a year.

Occasionally, the kids even shared their humble home with overnight guests — two cousins who would take to the streets after family fights or evictions.

Along came two more relatives—whether they were nephews, half-brothers, or more cousins, no one could say for sure. The bottom line was that all the kids needed a stable home.

They ranged in age from 12 to 17 and had banded together in sort of a survival unit. The older ones worked fast food and odd jobs; the younger ones worked when they could and went to school occasionally. They mutually shared good and bad times.

I often come across arrangements like this among kids from disfunctional families. Since they lack responsible parents, the kids take on the responsibility for one another.

It all sounds quite noble—the kind of tear-jerker stuff movies are made of. But in real life, these stories don't end like the movies—with the older kids finding perfect homes for their brothers and sisters with wonderful people taking them in as well.

There aren't too many people willing to take teenagers into their homes, especially those with problems attached.

In addition to lots of "no happy endings" to their stories, young kids who are forced by life to grow up too fast lose themselves in the process.

To begin with, they are never really children. While other kids are swapping baseball cards or giggling about a valentine from that special someone, these kids are finding mom or dad missing or passed out or stalling the landlord for the rent.

The kids usually blame themselves for their situation because often their parents do a good job laying guilt trips on them. "If it weren't for you" is the lullaby they heard since birth.

Not too many years into their childhood, these kids realize they can count on nothing. They can trust no one. They plan emergency exits for all they do—if Mom or Dad doesn't show, I'll get a ride with Jimmy; if there's no food, I'll steal some.

They become masters of manipulation, "con-children", adept enough to take on any professional con artist. They get smart, very street-smart. They learn the rules of survival, and they do what they need to do, often at the expense of their identities and their lives.

Then reality and sometimes the law begin to catch up with them. They can't earn enough money to live on. Their parents steal or "borrow" their meager earnings for a bottle of cheap wine. They begin selling drugs or sex to stay alive, and their parents even encourage them.

"People have a soft heart for a kid," a parent told one of our kids as he taught him the finer points of begging.

A lot of our kids take drugs or use sex to keep from feeling alive. When they sell, use, abuse, or take enough, their lives are over—in a prison or a grave — so often . . . all before their 16th birthday.

I'm often asked—what kind of parents would do things like this to their own kids? The answer is all kinds. Some of the parents obviously have more than a few screws loose from the start. Or are so fried out from years of drug use, they can't function at all.

The majority, however, are not all that bad all of the time. And maybe this is worse. They fade in and out of jobs, moods, and their kids' lives, leaving their kids with neither consistent affection nor abuse to count on.

It's almost like the slot machines in Las Vegas, the way many of our kids grow up. Most of the time, there's no pay off. Dad or mom is drunk, drugged, abusive, and unemployed. That's the status quo. Poverty and all the problems that come with it are the family's bread and butter.

Once in a while, though, Lady Luck makes a call and visits the crumbling family. The parent lands a job for a few months. A relative dies and leaves them a thousand or so bucks. The horses pay off, or someone wins the pot in a poker game. Maybe someone even makes it to an AA meeting.

The parent announces, "Things are going to be different from now on!"

And they are.

The rent gets paid, and there's food to eat. The kid isn't hit around. The parent says, "I'm sorry. You're a good kid. I love you." Maybe not with those words, but somehow. Maybe with a few candy bars or gifts. Maybe with a trip to the movies.

Timidly, the kid starts to believe in mom or dad again. The family starts looking like a real family instead of people linked together by genes and trouble.

Then, one day, the kid comes home from school with a good mark on a paper or a special art picture. Bursting with pride, he or she rounds the last flight of stairs. The yelling from their apartment fills the hall. The paper gets wadded up and tossed into the gutter as the kid takes to the streets until things quiet down. And after a few emotional roller coaster rides like these, the kid won't bother bringing home papers, feelings, or anything else.

It's easier to detach. Play dead. They can't hurt you that way. Their family slot machine pays off so seldom, they stop putting in nickels.

Are these kids worse off, or better off, because of this

inconsistent kind of nurturing and love? I don't know.

I can only tell you how much they suffer, for many years with us, and for many years afterwards. Their wounds are deep, reaching spiritually, emotionally, and often physically into their very fragile souls. Some scars will never go away.

Their parents have given them the same kind of love they knew growing up. Most likely, their kids will continue the legacy. After all, it's a family affair.

Chapter Seven

THE PRICE OF LOVE

Bill's life story really began a few years before he was born. It was back in the 1960s—that idyllic time of ideals, peace, and love.

Bill's mom was a young, bright, and beautiful college student from a well-to-do family. She plunged into the anti-materialism that was popular on college campuses and went on to become a full-fledged hippie. Unfortunately, she also jumped into the free love and drugs that guided flower children down their primrose paths. She was a disgrace to her family.

When she became pregnant, her family had taken about as much as they could. At that point, she was disowned and cut off from the family finances.

She made it to Florida, where she had Bill and continued onward with her free-spirit, heavy-drug lifestyle. Their homes were a series of communes, and occasionally a rundown apartment or flophouse room.

She kept on the move a lot, working alternately as a drug pusher or prostitute to make ends meet. And, true to the old adage, she eventually "came home again" to Chicago.

Her family remained bitter and refused to see or help her or her son Bill in any way. She had made her bed. Let her lie in it.

That's the bad news. But there was some good news, too. By some stroke of fate, Bill was a normal, very bright child. He loved his mother, and, in her own way, she loved him beyond all telling. The two were inseparable.

Granted, it was not a healthy parent-child relationship because the mother was too unstable and drugged to be counted on very much. But his mom was the only person Bill had. He wasn't about to give her up or to give up on her.

By the time they hit Chicago, Bill was 14 and three years behind in school because of moving around so much. He was picked up for stealing a candy bar one day. This incident opened up to the world the painfully sick can of worms his life had become.

Bill came to live at Mercy Boys' Home. His mom stayed in Chicago. Periodically we'd hear from her. Once, after a lag of a few weeks of no word, I set out to track her down.

I found the flophouse where she was living. But just an hour before I arrived, they found her body. The deputy coroner said she was probably an unclaimed corpse at the morgue. Bill and I made the trip there together.

Understandably he was very upset and blamed himself for her death.

"If only I just stayed with her," he said. His voice trailed off into memories that he didn't want to share.

The self-inflicted responsibility and guilt he felt for her death would be with him a long, long while.

I contacted Bill's grandparents and told them of

their daughter's death. After a family consultation, the grandfather told me he would "take care of" the funeral. He would make arrangements for the service and the cremation. He would not, he emphatically underlined, be responsible for a burial, but would "see that the boy received his mother's ashes".

I told him that Mercy Boys' Home would pay for the ashes to be interred.

The service was one of the saddest I've ever attended. Bill and I sat on one side of the church. His grandparents, uncles, aunts, and other relatives—none of whom he had ever met—gathered in a tight pack on the other side. Few of them made the slightest gesture of even acknowledging our presence.

Somewhere into the service, Bill began crying. I put my arm around him. Tears began to well up in my eyes too. I truly regretted his mom had wasted her life. But I grieved for Bill and all he had missed. I was angry most of all for the injustice of his situation. He didn't ask to be born, but he was loyal.

The minister gave a glowing, carefully rehearsed eulogy which went far beyond accentuating the positive. He talked about the kind of girl that the family had wanted their daughter to be, as no doubt he had been requested to do.

"That's not the way she was at all," Bill told me later. "Why'd they lie?"

I could only grip his shoulder a bit tighter.

After the service, as relatives escaped to their BMW's, Rolls, and other appropriate wheeled symbols of affluence, Bill's grandfather began walking toward us.

We were getting into my car, which was definitely outclassed and unwelcome in that neighborhood, as were Bill and I.

The grandfather waited until Bill was in the car and then approached me.

"What you are doing for my daughter's son is very charitable," he said. "But under the circumstances we cannot play a part in his care. I'm certain you can understand."

He finished with a polite, half-hearted smile, started to extend his hand, but then drew it back. Somehow I was stoical.

Noticing my less than enthusiastic expression, he repeated, "You do understand, of course . . . ," and backed away.

That was the last Bill or I saw or heard of his mother's family.

Bill asked me to get in touch with friends of his mother. They had lived with them in Florida. He took her ashes and visited the friends. Together they scattered them over the ocean. He felt his mom was at peace at last.

I have a hard time telling this story. Naturally, my heart goes out to Bill. He was an innocent victim in the whole thing. But I have an especially hard time understanding his grandparents.

On the other hand, I didn't meet Bill's mom until her life had pretty much passed the point of no return.

I don't know the extent of the pain she had caused her parents. I don't know how hard they tried before giving up. And I am well aware that a troubled kid can cause intense pain for those who care about their welfare. But to turn their backs on their daughter's son hits my solar plexus. I best be silent.

In just the short few years a kid is at Mercy Boys' Home, I experience the tumultuous ride of adolescence in full force numerous times. I think we're making headway with a kid; then the kid does a tailspin and goes back four steps. We get one problem settled and enroll the kid in a good school. The kid wants to drop out.

Kids have come to me with tears in their eyes.

"Father, you're a good guy and everything, but I just can't hack it here."

"Sorry, Father, the Home's great for most of the kids. Just not me. It won't work for me. I've got to move on."

Then, sadly, I admit to myself—we can't help them all. It hurts me, I suppose, in much the same way that it hurts a parent to lose a son or daughter to gangs, drugs, or undesirable friends.

There are simply no easy answers. Not at our Home, and not in the home of parents who love their kids enough to still care, no matter what.

This word "love" we toss around so lightly these days—what is it really?

Hanging in there when we think we'll be disappointed?

Hanging in there when a kid doesn't deserve another chance?

Hanging in there because a kid never had a chance?

I think it's all these things, and loads more.

Every day, I discover more nuances of its meaning from our kids. And after all these years, there is only one thing I know for sure—I never saw a kid succeed without getting love from somewhere.

It's always best if parents are the ones who give kids the love they need. But, lacking that, I am comforted to know that Mercy Boys' Home can fill in the gaps sometimes and give roots to my boys and girls.

Chapter Eight

BETWEEN APPOINTMENTS

From the top of his carefully manicured hair and nails, through his impeccably tailored suit, down to his expensive-looking shoes, Mr. Success projected an image of having made it—and made it well.

He came to see me between his appointments. He was in Chicago just for the day. One of his clients cancelled. That gave him an hour or two to kill. He decided to come looking for the kid that "used to be" his son.

I say "used to be" because Mark had been with us over a year by this time. Despite numerous attempts on Mark's part, he had never received any communication from his dad—the tanned Mr. Success who now stood before me. His dad had thrown him out and intended to keep the doors locked.

Mark was different from most of the kids at Mercy Boys' Home in that he had once been part of a so-called "normal" American family. He had a mom, a dad, a sister, a dog, a comfortable house in a prestigious suburb, rock posters on his bedroom wall, and all the video games and designer jeans that would fit into his walk-in closet.

Most likely, beneath this facade, the problems

which were to become part of Mark's later life were
there. They just never surfaced much. That's one
thing about having money—it can make denying
problems easier. It also gives the family more options
in dealing with them if they chose to do so.

In Mark's case, this decision was never made. It
was less stressful to just cover things up.

The turning point came when Mark's mom and
dad divorced. Mark became one of those kids-in-the-
middle nobody likes to talk about.

He lived with his mom for a while, but began
getting into trouble—first in school, and later on with
the police. He acknowledged he used a daily jolt of
marijuana and alcohol "to take the edge off" the
whole mess.

After an unsuccessful attempt with a counselor or
two, he moved in with his dad. By this time, dad had a
new wife—a much younger woman who just wasn't too
keen on taking in a troubled teenager, particularly since
there was their 3 year old baby daughter to think about.

Push came to shove several times. Eventually, Mark
split and followed the usual runaway's path—hitch-
hiking across the United States, stealing enough to
survive along the way, drifting in and out of temporary shelters and homes, experimenting with more
drugs here and there, attracting the attention of the
police, and eventually ending up in a Chicago juvenile
court where his crooked path was retraced and a
decision made.

His mom said she simply "couldn't handle him"—
her own life was in turmoil as it was. His dad said he

"didn't want Mark disrupting his new family".

Accordingly, Mark was branded "incorrigible" although he had never really done enough of anything to merit a permanent lock-up. After consultation, Mark and our staff and I mutually agreed to give one another a chance.

Mark settled in at the Home surprisingly well. As he continued his drug and alcohol recovery program, he began to lose some of the denial and bitterness that kept him so angry and charged up in years past.

Having given up on his mom, whom no one could locate anyway, Mark wrote to his dad. His letters came back marked "REFUSED." He tried calling a few times. He got either a phone message recorder or the new wife, but never a return call from his father.

Quite understandably, he reached the conclusion that his dad didn't care about him. I endorsed his thinking when his dad didn't return my calls or answer my letters on behalf of Mercy Boys' Home.

After talking it out again and again in his group sessions at the Home and with a psychiatrist, Mark finally began to move ahead with his goals and his life. The hurt was still there, but the wounds weren't gaping as much anymore. The scars faded a bit.

I knew all this. After living with these kids night and day, there's little that I don't know about them. Or for that matter that they don't know about me.

At times, miracles do happen, and here was one. Mark's dad had a business break and thought he'd fill it with a short visit with his son.

"I know he's here," said Mr. Success. "I get the

letters."

"Do you think it's really such a good idea after all this time?" I asked, skeptically.

"He *IS* my son," he said, indignantly.

"Oh, well, let's see. If Mark is your son, then you must be his father. But I'm bothered—because Mark never gets a birthday card or Christmas card from a dad. And a dad never answers his letters, or mine either," I interjected with a dose of sarcasm.

I know, I was not being Mr. Nice, and Mr. Success picked it up. He was no dummy. After some reciprocal verbal jousting, we got down to business.

"You want to spend a half-hour or so with Mark and then leave. Because it's convenient for you," I told him. "I don't think it's such a good idea for Mark. Because if that's all you want, once you leave, we'll have to spend the next several months trying to get Mark over the trauma of your visit.

"You can see him, but let's work out the preliminaries. Let me talk to him first. I'll tell him you're here."

With that, the dad cursed me, turned on his heel and walked out. He's never tried to contact his son again—even after Mark was out of college and on his own, and even after he had reestablished ties with his sister and mom.

Like the dad said to me during his visit, "the kid just didn't work out" for him. Actually my heart goes out to the father almost as much to the son.

This incident was one of those hard-to-call decisions that I have to make sometimes. Maybe I was wrong in not immediately letting the dad see Mark, but I don't think so. For kids like Mark, the trauma of love lost twice most probably would have been too much for him to take and would have endangered his entire recovery program.

In any event, I thought it was too great a risk to take at that time. And I never told Mark his dad had come by to see him.

I admit to having reacted too emotionally to Mark's dad. I guess it's part of caring too much sometimes about kids like Mark and all the kids who live with us.

Being in charge here doesn't mean I turn into a saint. In fact, I firmly believe that there is nothing more humbling than being around kids. They keep you honest. And kids like those living here can zero in on pretense with the radar of a stealth bomber.

After what they've been through, they'll learn to accept almost anything, even if it is being rejected by their parents. But you've got to keep your feet on the ground. My job, and the job of all of us here is to give our kids a new reality to focus on—a home and a family they can count on.

We do not judge kids by what happened *before* they got here. Though their past often dictates their behaviors, habits, defenses, and coping strategies, we start from square one—now, today. Their slate is clean as far as we're concerned.

Nor do we judge the parents and families of our kids. Though I have to admit my temper occasionally overrides my professionalism—as in the case of Mr.

Success—our basic approach to helping the families of our kids is the same as our approach to helping the kids: let's start over. Let's start with now, today.

It's a new day, and there's a lot to feel good about! That's my prayer each morning. And I do pray!

Chapter Nine

A CERTAIN SMILE

Many people think that, given the traumatic lives our kids have had, that there is a quiet, depressing atmosphere around them.

Such is not the case.

Most of our kids have an extraordinary sense of humor and a keen wit. They temper these with the ability to find the bright side of almost any circumstance. They like to embellish their stories with kindly sarcasm and animated gestures.

This enables them to deal with their problems in a manner which entertains, rather than disheartens others. Since the vast majority of them are people pleasers, they work hard to make others feel comfortable in their presence.

People like having people around who make them laugh. And our kids know this. A joke and a ready smile is an easy way to break the ice in uncomfortable situations.

Granted, their motives are not always pure. They may use humor and friendship as a way to manipulate or control.

For example, recently Andy was referred to me by one of the house parents for an infraction. He came in with a broad smile, joking and making light of the

incident in the hopes that I, too, would laugh about it
and forget the real reason for his visit.

It didn't work, not because I didn't appreciate his
efforts, but because I have had so many years to
prepare my defense.

I like a good laugh as much as the next one, but I'm
also good at ferreting out blarney when I need to.

When I confronted Andy with the truth, his "ha-
ha" quickly faded to anger and then tears. That's the
way feelings are with our kids, and, to some degree,
with adolescents in general.

Teenagers are creatures of extremes. Things are
"great," not "fine". Just as easily, they become "the
worst". And all of this overreacting seems to magnify
itself in troubled kids.

Thus, there's a lot of potential energy surfacing in the
course of a day at Mercy Boys' Home. Not all of it is
positive either. Trigger tempers are not uncommon
among our kids, and the fuel for ignition lurks behind
every misplaced book or borrowed item. Particularly
with our newcomers, an unintentional jostle or the
wrong words spoken in greeting are often seen as threats.

One of the things nearly every one of our kids has
to work on is finding acceptable ways to accept and
express anger. Learning to discuss things without fists
is a learned behavior. This is true even for our girls,
some of whom are quite good at scrapping if the
circumstance warrants it.

This applies to those kids who still have some life
and energy in them—even if it is coming out as
rebellion.

A more difficult type of kid to deal with is one so beaten by life that he or she has nearly totally withdrawn.

At first, these kids seem easier to handle than the rebels. They are usually quiet and polite. They cooperate without questioning. They attend school and do their chores without complaint. They rarely do anything to upset the status quo, making them like a breath of cool air in our hotly charged environment.

We had one kid—I'll call him Jim—who did not say one word, literally, for several months after his arrival. He ate, slept, and did all we asked him to do — but he would not talk to anyone.

I have to admit, with all that can go on in a "normal" day at Mercy Boys' Home, with so many teenagers under one roof, the contingent in Aftercare section, plus our Mercy Girls' Home, it's really tempting to leave kids like Jim alone. Yet we know that in the long run this would not be in their best interest. So, comfortable or not, we attempt to involve them actively in our program.

The peculiar thing that happens sometimes, as it did in Jim's case, is that as these kids begin to get better, their behavior begins to get worse. Jim, for example, turned into a regular hellion for a while.

This rapid rise to rebellion is usually a good sign with such kids because it means that they are moving out of their self-imposed isolation. As they start caring more about themselves, they begin to stand up for their rights and assert their independence.

Despite our efforts, however, some of our kids

never do begin to open up. Linda was one of our most striking failures in this regard.

Since I don't profess to be an expert on raising boys, I definitely put myself in the novice category when it comes to girls. For the most part, I am not involved in the daily activities of our girls. We have a fine staff of professionals who handle things quite well in our Mercy Girls' Home.

Like Jim in his early days with us, Linda was no trouble. True, she did absolutely nothing in school because she usually slept. That's what she did in her free time at Mercy Girls' Home, too. And when she was awake, she was little more than a body with a vacant smile.

A "certain smile" I like to call it, because I have come across it many times in withdrawn kids. It is a haunting smile, almost as if these kids are in on some vast secret of the universe that the rest of us don't have access to.

It's not a real smile. There's no energy or feeling behind it. Rather, it's more like a permanent reflex, a plastered on, passive response to all that has gone before.

In Linda's case, it was sexual abuse by her father and several other men that may have precipitated her tuning out on life. Her sisters were also abused, but somehow they were not as affected as she was.

The life had been sucked out of her as surely as if she were dead. And just as surely as death, there would be no change unless something drastic happened.

After a long while with us and numerous attempts

at different therapies, we couldn't reach her and had to refer Linda to an agency where she could receive more intense psychiatric help than we were able to give her. At last check, she was institutionalized and would most likely remain so for the rest of her life.

Where was the real Linda, the little girl with long braids and an upturned nose we saw in her early school pictures? In a world of dreams, perhaps a better world than the one she had come to know.

I hope it is less painful there for her, and I hope the same for all the kids I meet who have drifted too far from reality for us to help.

Kids like Jim and Linda, and the many others who have followed them, have taught me that I must look far deeper than a joke or a wistful smile to find the real person. Here, and in life generally, that's a good way to approach people.

Chapter Ten

GETTING READY TO FLY

I like to think of our work at Mercy Boys' Home as preparing our girls and boys for flight. Not that I really want them to leave. Like any parent, I have conflicting feelings about parting with kids who have been such a predominant part of my life. Most of our kids stay with us for many years, and there's a lot of history packed into those days, highlighted with some tears and laughs.

The Mercy Boys' Home staff and I have watched them grow from troubled, chunky, or lanky, out-of-proportion thirteen year olds to attractive, responsible men and women. We've worried with them about having enough high school credits to graduate, shared the joy of getting a driver's license, and soothed feelings on a Christmas Day when no one came to visit them.

And what I want for these kids is no different from what any concerned parent wants. I want them to be able to go out into the world as healthy, happy, independent adults.

When I first began at Mercy Boys' Home, I had a rather simple view of the task before me. If we supplied food, clothing, shelter, education, and a large dosage of love, the final product would be a mature adult. What I found out was—to use a phrase I picked up from the kids—"It don't work that way".

I qualify that by saying—it doesn't usually work that way.

For most of our kids, living as part of our family is as close to a stable environment as most ever had. Though our kids often make great strides in overcoming their problems in a short period of time, they hardly ever catch up with kids who have grown up in a consistent, loving family atmosphere.

Nevertheless, our kids, like everyone else's, legally become adults at age 18. And officially, our residential care should end at that time.

I say "officially" because anyone who has ever had anything to do with kids knows it's not that easy. Few 18 year olds can face life on their own.

To begin with, most decent jobs today demand either a college degree or technical training—and what kid can totally support himself or herself while pursuing an education, considering the cost of education today?

About 60 percent of our kids do attend college, and the other 40 percent usually enter career tracks requiring some type of advanced technical education or training. So our involvement in their lives, though a bit less, is still very necessary.

Then there's a question of how they will learn to live independently.

Unlike the TV commercials, our kids don't have moms to tell them how to sort colored from white clothes and what the water temperature should be.

In addition, many have the burden of never having had things like clean clothes and regular meals until they came to live with us.

One of our kids, at age 13, was still eating with his hands for the simple reason that no one ever taught him not to. He saw no reason to bother with a fork.

From the time he was very young, meals at his house were a catch-as-catch-can affair. If food was in the refrigerator or cabinet, everybody took what they wanted. If there was no food, everybody went hungry, ate at a friend's home, hustled money for food, or stole enough junk food to get by.

Our goal with kids like this—kids who enter the race of life long after the rest of the runners have taken off —remains essentially the same as it always is. We want to help our kids develop the skills they need to be on their own. Only the timing changes.

Sometimes a kid's past experiences are so sporadic and traumatic, and they come to us so late, the best thing we can shoot for is to pray that we won't make them worse than they are.

Although some people might see this attitude as negative and defeatist, I see it as a more positive light.

Most of our kids are the products of a lot of "band-aid" help. They hurt physically, mentally, emotionally, and spiritually from the depths of their being.

But instead of intensive care and major surgery, what most of them receive is help of the "quick-fix" variety.

Give them shelter for a couple nights, a new set of clothes, and a hot meal, and send them on. Or give them counseling, an unrealistic few hours with a social worker, psychologist, psychiatrist, a school counselor to try to undo a lifetime of problems and neglect.

In most cases, the kid's family is not involved in either of these emergency approaches, so whatever headway is made is quickly undone when the kid returns to the setting which caused his or her problems in the first place.

We don't use generic solutions to solve specific problems. Instead, we take a broader, longer view and really try to sustain whatever care we are able to provide.

Our kids have been let down so much in life by so many people, we don't want to be just another in their long list of failures. And we don't want to duplicate the emergency services provided by other agencies— like shelters for runaways, or drug and alcohol treatment centers.

When a kid lives with us, we make a commitment that we will do everything we can to ensure his success and growth. Whether the kid has medical insurance or the ability to pay is not an issue. And I don't have to tell you, caring for kids is never cheap. You just know that kids like ours cost even more.

Thus far, thanks to the understanding and generosity of our donors, we have been able to keep our doors open for 103 years.

We could do it cheaper, but our program would provide little more than a temporary change of scenery. We could service more kids, but our facilities and resources would become so strained, and our energies so scattered, no kid would receive the kind of individual attention, care, and love needed. I know we can't save them all.

So, we'd be right back to where we started when our

kids came to us, patting them on the head and putting them back on the street at age 18, still hurting, still unskilled, still unemployable, and still lacking maturity.

In our 103-year history, after serving more than 16,000 kids, we have never done this, and we don't plan to.

Even after our kids leave our Home, our doors remain open to them. They can always return to visit or to share a meal with us, and our staff is always available if they want to talk to someone. Any number of young people still lean on us.

Also, for as long as our help is needed, we are in touch with our kids through our extensive Aftercare programs.

For those not quite ready to "make the break" with us, or who cannot afford to live on their own, we have an independent living program in a separate section of Mercy Boys' Home. Organized around apartment-like facilities, the boys share a kitchen plus housekeeping chores, but assume greater freedom and responsibility for their lives. Most have full or part time jobs and are involved in some type of educational program.

Our second phase of Aftercare goes a step beyond this. Boys live in apartments away from Mercy Boys' Home, but retain some of their ties to us.

Developing an effective Aftercare program for Mercy Girls' Home is our latest project.

Aftercare is a way of extending the love, care, and affection of our family to those past the age of 18— another way to give them the security of the family roots and ties that most of them missed growing up.

It's simply a safety net for our kids.

At Mercy Boys' Home and Mercy Girls' Home, giving our kids roots doesn't mean that they will be able to trace their ancestors back or that they will have an intense pride or fond memories of their early childhood years. What it does mean is that they stop blowing about like tumbleweed across the mainstream of life.

They, too, have a family who loves and cares about them. They, too, have a family who stands by them. They, too, have the self-esteem, confidence, and skills to care for themselves and to give to others less fortunate. Through their association with us, they have become part of our large and happy family. Their family is "us"!

For over one hundred years, Mercy Boys' Home has opened its doors to abandoned, abused and orphaned kids.

This is how our dining room looked back in 1933. Times change, but kids' appetites don't!

Seems like my kids are always hungry! Thanks to friends like you, they now get 3 square meals a day.

*In addition to food, clothing and shelter,
homeless kids need professional counseling.
Mercy Boys' Home provides the best.*

Every kid needs a friendly spot where he can enjoy a good book. At Mercy Boys' Home, we make sure he has one.

Every kid at Mercy Boys' Home must attend school. So homework is something we take very seriously.

Team sports are an important part of life at the Home.

Experiencing the great outdoors is important to our kids' personal growth ... some of them have never been out of the city before!

Some of our caring friends made donations to help us purchase a monument to remember eight Mercy boys buried in unmarked graves in a potter's field.

All of our kids learn the value of a good day's work.

I'm really proud of these kids. They turned their lives around and received scholarships to college.

Mercy Girls' Home gives these girls a safe and secure family where they are loved and wanted.

Even though the holidays are difficult for the kids, they still love to bring home the traditional Christmas tree.

Thousands of troubled boys have climbed the steps of Mercy Boys' Home. For each one, it's the first step toward a better life.

WINGS

"They that hope in the Lord
will renew their strength,
they will soar as with eagles' wings;
They will run and not grow weary,
walk and not grow faint."

Isaiah 40:31*

*Taken from the New American Bible
Copyright © 1970, Confraternity of Christian Doctrine,
Washington, D.C. Used with permission.

Chapter Eleven

HEALING THE WOUNDS

Joey asked me to go with him to his dad's funeral. I would have offered to go anyway, but I was honored that he trusted and respected me enough to ask. He had only been at the Home for about five months.

His dad was an alcoholic who died of cirrhosis after years of struggling alternately with the disease and recovery programs. He left this world knowing that his son would be taken care of with us.

When we arrived at the church, many of Joey's relatives were there, but not his mom. She had deserted the family when Joey was three. No one had heard from her since.

"This is my 'father'," he said, when introducing me.

He smiled when he said it and beamed as if I were really someone special in his life. I was surprised being introduced as his "father", but it made me feel good.

Funerals are seldom happy occasions. Yet, sometimes, like with Joey, the death of a parent brings out the best in our kids. Through death, sometimes they are freed from the guilt which has held them captive.

Maybe it's the finality and the shock of seeing someone dead whom they cared about, or whom they struggled to care about their entire lives.

Moms or dads who abuse and use, neglect and

ignore, and love and hate their kids often assume a bigger-than-life size importance in their kids' lives. In some cases, these parents are nearly up there with God in omnipotence—at least, in the minds of their kids.

Although this is almost inconceivable for those of us who were blessed with loving, rational parents, it is a perfectly logical reaction for a child raised in an abusive home.

The parent-child relationship begins at birth, and, in the case of the mother, from the time of conception. Given the innocence and immaturity of the child when the abuse begins, the child assumes that mom and dad are okay. But the child sees himself as not okay.

This mindset stays with a child, often for life, causing problems with self-esteem, confidence, maturity, and a host of other areas.

The child may intuitively suspect something is wrong, yet because of his or her total dependence on the parent for survival, deny these feelings. Such feelings never go away. The child grows up thinking there is some deep, horrible secret that no one must ever know about the family. The parent may even reinforce this by repeatedly admonishing the child never to tell anyone anything about what goes on in their home.

The secret becomes so awful, so overwhelming, that the child neither knows nor wants to know exactly what it is. But the threat of that secret is strong enough to dictate every thought, word, action, and feeling in the child's life for many years.

After years of submerging and denying feelings and everything else, some bizarre coping mechanisms begin to develop in the child. These tend to "peak out" in adolescence—a time of ups and downs for even the most normal of kids.

Healing, if it comes at all, takes place in stages. With help, many of the kids come to grips with the gaping wounds in their life. Having consistent love, affection, and limits does wonders. So does having someone they can trust.

For starters, this is what we try to accomplish. Essentially, it's "closing the gaping wounds" by placing the kid in a stable atmosphere where real healing can begin.

As a kid gains some sense of self-worth, we move ahead with other steps in the healing process.

Although healing in our kids is an individual thing that defies time restrictions and master plans, there does seem to be a process many of them go through.

I've never seen all of this documented anywhere in professional literature. In fact, I've never even written it down before. But it seems to work for the benefit of the kids. Since I'm a pragmatist at heart, that's good enough for me.

Once their "settling in" with us is over and done with—and this can take almost the entire time the kid is with us—we introduce our kids to some new ways of looking at things.

First, we show and tell them that the way they have lived is not the only way, and may not have been the best way, to live.

Second, we help them deal with their past by coming to grips with their parents, their own mistakes and failures, or whatever else is blocking their physical, mental, emotional, and spiritual growth.

Third, whenever possible, we keep them connected with their families—parents, grandparents, brothers, sisters, cousins, aunts, uncles, or whomever. We feel their families, good, bad or indifferent, are a part of themselves they cannot go on denying.

Then, too, there is always the chance for positive changes in the family. Because of this, we try to keep the family involved in our programs. For, try as they might, and deny as they might, our kids are, have been, and will always be, members of their biological families.

Fourth, we encourage our kids to stop licking their wounds. They must learn to forgive themselves and all who are, or were, dear to them. They must accept what is, and was, change what they can, and move ahead.

And finally, we encourage them to dream, or at least show them a few goals they can shoot for in their years ahead. I see this as a very important part of our work. I am convinced that we must start our kids thinking this way. If our kids have something positive to motivate them, even if they still bear the scars of their childhood years, they'll usually turn out okay.

Mercy Boys' Home exists not just to keep troubled kids off the streets, but to see that they will stay off the streets once they are on their own. We are here to help give them wings for their future.

Chapter Twelve

PUTTING THE PAST TO REST

If I make what we do sound easy and prescriptive, I don't mean to. Healing is not a passive process; it's hard work—both for the kids and my staff. Our kids have to want to heal as much as we want them to heal. And still, despite our joint efforts, not all kids "heal" the way we'd like.

Paul was one of those.

True, he had a lot to overcome in life. As the oldest of three children, he bore the brunt of the family's problems. The family disintegrated while his brother and sister were very young. Paul came to Mercy Boys' Home at the tender age of fourteen.

His father was an alcoholic. His mom died of drinking. Emotionally depressed, his grandmother took her own life. It was a lot to deal with for any kid.

He did the best he could, and seemed to succeed. He finished high school and college and landed a good job. This was not too surprising since he was bright, handsome, and had a pleasant, outgoing personality.

In fact, his brother and sister were bright, beautiful kids, but they were also fragile. And so was Paul.

His problems, however, were not very apparent to the outside observer. Like many "oldest" children in typical dysfunctional families, Paul became an adult at an early age. He assumed responsibility for his brother and sister, became an overachiever in all he did, and kept his real problems buried deep inside.

Occasionally, I'd see hints that all was not well. His laughter often lacked conviction and sounded hollow—as if he was laughing only because he knew that was what others expected of him.

Then, too, he refused to attend his mom's funeral. I was concerned about his reaction. But there was nothing I or anyone else could do.

After Paul left the Home and got his own apartment, I didn't see him again until he was some four months into his new job. I met him in an odd place, the cemetery. I was visiting a grave site with one of our kids from the Home. As we made our way back to our car, a shiny, new automobile slowed down. At the wheel was Paul, who greeted us with his usual warm smile. He was with Carol, his youngest sister.

"Guess you want to know what I'm doing here?" he questioned. He told me that he had taken an advance on his salary to buy grave markers for his mother's and grandmother's graves. He was at the cemetery to see if they were in place yet.

It was his own way of finishing off his grieving process. That day, some several years after the funerals of his mother and his grandmother, Paul had finally laid them to rest emotionally in his own life.

He was finally ready to heal the bruised and wounded parts of himself that he had put down for so

long. And maybe somewhere deep within, he'd find
the little boy who never had a chance to be a kid. I
hoped so.

Chapter Thirteen

NOBODY'S FAMILY, NOBODY'S CHILD

Some of our kids do more than try to bury the past. They try to eliminate it — to erase it completely. They are so desperate to forget what their hurt has been, they don't even want to keep their names.

It's not a question of having some offbeat name and wanting to change it to something less noticeable. They want to get rid of their last names whether common or not, and for a few kids, their first names as well.

Once they turn 18, it's surprisingly easy for these kids to invent a new identity—superficially, at least—by christening themselves via the courts with a new name.

Having never been tempted to make such a radical change myself, I thought it impossible. But all they need to do is swear that they are not making the change to defraud anyone in any way and have their Social Security number and other permanent records transferred to their new name.

Sometimes the new name is enough to get them started on a whole wave of changes towards a new and better life as adults. Sometimes, too, it can produce some peculiar twists of its own, as in the case of Sam.

Sam was so wounded by the abandonment and

abuse he suffered during his childhood years, he wanted to erase the fact that his parents, his family, and his past ever existed.

When he was old enough, he took a new name and eliminated as much of his history from the records and his memory as circumstances would allow. It took me awhile to get used to calling Ron by his new name, "Sam." I mixed up Sam and Ron quite a few times in the beginning.

After a few years paying his dues at a few low paying jobs, he decided what he really wanted to do with his life. He applied for a job as a police officer. Despite his excellent health, job record, and good grades, he was never even called in for an interview.

It was a blow harsh enough to burst the "happy ever after" bubble he had created for himself.

I thought about it for a while, and talked to other members of our staff. None of us could figure it out, any more than Sam could.

Mostly to satisfy my own curiosity, I contacted a friend I knew at the Police Academy. After my many years at Mercy Boys' Home, obviously I knew quite a few police officers. Yet I didn't want to use undue influence to get Sam on the force.

First of all, I knew he truly had more than enough going for him to be accepted in the Academy. In addition, it was important to Sam to prove to himself that he could do it on his own.

When my police friend did some checking, he discovered that Sam's name change was the culprit. Understandably, the committee reviewing Sam's application thought he might have something to hide and didn't bother to pursue the matter further.

So complete was Sam's denial of his history on his application, he also did not indicate that he had lived at Mercy Boys' Home. This left even more time gaps and unanswered questions.

Once the reason for the name change was brought to light, Sam was accepted into the Academy. He came by to see me one day, ramrod straight and proud as he could be of his uniform.

His visit was as much of a formal thanks to the Mercy Boys' Home as it was to me. His words, of course, never indicated that. He talked about his work, and his new apartment, and a girl who had become special to him. He talked a lot, but never really said too much about anything.

I understood. Most of our kids find it as difficult to express positive emotions as they do to express negative ones.

But I knew. And he knew I knew.

I guess it's the same between children and their natural parents. Sometimes you don't need words to get the job done.

Chapter Fourteen

DON'T LOOK BACK

"Father, with as many kids as your Homes have helped, you must have an alumni association out of this world," people question me on occasion.

But surprisingly, we don't—or maybe not so surprisingly.

It isn't that our kids are not grateful for what the Mercy Boys' Home have done for them. They are.

Many do stay in touch with us and donate time and money to our Home when they are able to. Some are active in our "big brother-big sister" volunteer program as well.

This "internal" support is doubly appreciated by the staff and me because of the positive effect it has on our boys and girls.

Often, just hearing success stories for an hour or so from someone who's been there, and sharing experiences does more for a kid than we can accomplish in months.

We do have a newsletter which former residents receive to keep them informed of what's happening. Periodically, we have get-togethers. Then, too, each of our kids knows he or she can drop by at any time. This is home.

But some of our kids we do lose. I'm not sure if I

know exactly why, but I'm not particularly upset that it happens.

Judging from the comments I hear, a lot of these kids are suffering so greatly when they come to us, they resist keeping any part of that hurt in their lives. When they leave us, a painful chapter in their lives closes shut.

Fairly often, however, these kids drift back into our lives—usually when their own lives have settled down for a long enough period that they are strong enough and ready to take another look at who and where they've been.

Not a week goes by that someone doesn't come by or call and tell me that he once lived here. Some in their seventies write to us regularly as family.

Not long ago a man came by with his young sons. They were in Chicago on vacation. He had never told his kids that he had spent five years of his life with us.

"That time was such a hurting experience. I never looked back until today," he told me.

Another time, a man stopped by on his way home from work. He worked at a restaurant less than a mile from the Home and passed by at least twice a day for several years. He had lived here twenty years ago.

"When I left," he said, "I said to myself, 'Don't ever look back.' "

Experiences like these mean a lot to me. Though we want our kids to always feel close to us as part of our Mercy Home family, I don't begrudge any of them the freedom to decide when, and whether, to return.

Each kid needs to find his or her own way, in his or

her own time.

If we'd done our job right, giving our kids "wings" doesn't mean they have to fly in formation. Sometimes, it's only by soaring alone that a kid can reach new heights.

Chapter Fifteen

BREAKING THE CYCLE

I don't remember many scientific facts from my school days,—mostly because a lot of what I learned they have now either proven false or elaborated on so much that what I knew isn't worth remembering.

One of the things I do remember, that I think is still true, is that whatever is in motion tends to stay in motion.

The reason this has stayed with me longer than other facts is that I see so many examples of it in my work.

It goes back, too, to the old truism—as the twig is bent, so grows the tree.

Kids are like that. Usually, the way they are raised is the way they stay. And the way they stay is the way they raise their kids.

Poverty ... abuse ... alcoholism ... violence ... unemployment ... debt ... crime ... hopelessness ... powerlessness—and many other problems—tend to perpetuate themselves in families in much the same way as the legacies which healthier and more affluent parents leave their children.

Perhaps one of the greatest challenges we face in our work is breaking the cycle that has become the character of a kid's family.

Many times, if we can get a good thing going in a kid, the good spreads, not only to the kid's family but to the family he or she will have someday.

Our main concern, of course, is helping the kid get through the teenage years. We know we've succeeded when the kid leaves us as a self-sufficient, responsible adult. Successes beyond that I see as pure miracles.

Rick was one of these.

To know his family was to know a history of losing. There hadn't been a father around for generations. Rick's mom, his grandmother, and his great grandmother had the same life. They each had a child out of wedlock in their early teens, and quickly followed with several others. They spent their lives in abject poverty struggling to raise their kids.

Before coming to the Home, Rick had a good start on continuing the family pattern. He fathered a child at age fifteen. The girl involved was eighteen years old, and she wanted to keep the baby. Her family reluctantly agreed to help, but was absolutely against her having anything more to do with Rick.

Rick came to live with us, not solely because of this indiscretion, but because his own family situation had deteriorated even more with the neglect of his mother.

He lived with us the rest of his teen years, and made great headway sorting through his problems. After he left us, he set out to find the son he had never seen.

The path was easy enough to follow. The girl had

done little that was constructive in the ensuing years, and eventually had broken ties with her family. When Rick found her, she was very ill and severely addicted to drugs. A state agency was in the process of having her child taken away from her because of neglect. That child was his son!

Rick assumed responsibility for the care of his young son, and went on to become an excellent father. Eventually, he married a lovely woman. They now have two more children of their own.

As a family, they are not wealthy. But I doubt you could find a happier quintet.

I'm proud of Rick for a lot of reasons, mostly because he didn't take the easy way out, and because he broke the cycle of poverty and misfortune he grew up in.

It isn't often that we can help take one of our kids that far. But when I see Rick, his wife and their three kids together, I'm glad we tried.

Chapter Sixteen

REACHING OUT AGAIN

I don't like to admit this it, but some of our kids can be mighty selfish at times. Maybe protective is a better word.

They like to hoard the little treasures they have collected—whether it be money, a few paltry possessions, or themselves.

I understand why this is so.

Most of their lives, they've only had things taken away from them. So when they have a chance to be in control, they take advantage of the situation.

Parents tell me most kids are like this at some point in their lives. After witnessing two year olds fighting over a plastic pail in a sand box—both from homes with loving parents—I guess this is true.

The kids at Mercy Boys' Home and Mercy Girls' Home just take longer to outgrow the tendency.

It's hard to be a giver when you've been raised by takers.

And it's hard to risk reaching out again when you've had your efforts ridiculed and rejected continually. In short, taking a chance on people again is a hard part of "earning your wings." But some of our kids do make it . . . kids like Larry.

Larry quite frankly said he hated women when he

came to live with us. His mom had been a pretty sorry example of femininity. She was abusive, cruel, manipulative, and controlling. As Larry's only relative, she had a tremendous effect on him.

He grew up resenting her abuse, guilt trips, and domination. Unfortunately along the way Larry ran into a few other women who reinforced his negative view.

Nevertheless, during his years at the Home, he became quite close to one of the Sisters who help out here. All of us were happy to see this positive relationship developing.

Over the years, Sister became Larry's confidant and heroine. She became, for all practical purposes, the mom Larry wanted but never had.

As he prepared to leave us, Larry wanted to do something special for her—to give her a gift as a remembrance of him.

Embarrassed and sheepish, he came to me. I had never seen him so nervous.

"I don't know," said this lanky, six-foot-two kid holding out a bottle of cologne. "Do you think this is ok to give to a nun?"

"You mean Sister Joan?" I asked him.

He nodded.

"This is the first present I've ever given a woman," he said.

"I think it will be just fine," I told him. "I think she'll like it a lot."

After building up his courage for several days, Jim gave Sister his gift.

She was quite touched, and wanted to do something for him as well. Sister Joan went to her office and got an afghan which one of our donors had made. It was a beautiful thing—hand-crocheted in an intricate design in our school colors.

When we received it, Sister Joan had said to me, "It's just too nice to take a chance that it might end up getting tossed around. I'd like to save it for a someone special."

It was this afghan that Sister gave Larry, someone special.

"Will you write to thank the lady who made it and tell her I gave it to you?" she asked him.

He picked up the afghan and held it to his face, almost like a young child fondling a favorite blanket.

"It will be my warm remembrance of the people who make this Home possible," he said.

For Larry, his first experience reaching out again worked out well. He continued his college education while with us and started his career a stronger, better, and more compassionate person for having had a shaky start in life.

I wish it were in my power to make all of our kids' "reaching out" experiences like this. Sadly, it is not the story of everyone.

Some of our kids never do develop the security needed to try reaching out to others. A number of our boys and girls never marry, never have children, and never seem to establish close loving relationships with anyone. They have been just too damaged.

The lack of love and trust they experienced as

children keeps them suspicious and protective throughout their lives.

That doesn't mean they aren't successful. They are fine, wonderful people as adults.

But, in spite of their successes, they remain the ultimate losers in their failure to risk friendship and love again. Most of the time, they continue their lives feeling much like they have throughout their lives— very cheated and alone.

We try, of course, to change this in the days they are with us. Each of our kids has a staff member who serves as a personal advocate and friend in addition to the concern and love we try to show all of the kids.

Sometimes, it's not enough. But on the long shot that it will be, we'll keep on trying.

Chapter Seventeen

ONE FACE IN THE CROWD

It was hot, muggy Friday in late July, and "The El"—Chicago's name for our mass transit system—was crowded. Rush hour was just beginning, and I felt fortunate to find a seat.

I was tired after a long day of meetings and tired after an especially heavy schedule that week.

I wanted to relax. I wanted to get home. Most of all, I didn't want to see another kid or to hear about any kid's problems until I got there, and maybe not even then.

We had a crisis that week with one of the kids at the Home. I was feeling down-and-out about the situation. After months of working with him, we found out he had had a slip in his recovery and was using drugs again. He wasn't sure he wanted to stay with us.

A woman sat down next to me. Don't ask how, but she remembered me from a brief clip she had seen about Mercy Boys' Home on the T.V. news a week or so before.

"You're Father Close, aren't you?" she said. "You're the one who takes kids in."

For a moment, I considered denying my identity because I knew by the tone of her voice that she was going to have a lot to say. That's one thing I've learned through my years here—they don't ask if you're the one who takes kids in unless they know some who need a place to stay.

True to form, she started telling me about her nephew. She'd help him herself. Only she had a "kind of" sick husband and three kids of her own to take care of.

The nephew was her sister's son.

"Fortunately, it's her only child," she declared. "My sister's a real mess. I think she's crazy even if she is my sister."

She went on to describe the boy's home life, which was definitely not of the "Father Knows Best" vintage portrayed on TV. Her sister was unemployed and now into drugs. The man she lived with—not the boy's father—was also into drugs and out of a job.

And now her nephew was using them.

"He's a real mess," she said. "He's failing every subject in school and never goes half the time. None of them ever eat. They're all thin as rails and filthy looking. I'm ashamed to even have them come to visit. It's embarrassing to have the neighbors see them.

"Well, anyway, about Joey—that's his name, Joey—he's fifteen—he called me up. He wants to come and live with me. He wants to get off drugs and even went to some meetings or something. But he knows he can't make it if he stays there.

"Like I said, I want to help him, only I got no place for him. Besides, my husband hates my sister and that whole bunch. And he's still my husband. He thinks Joey'll ruin our kids. So, what I thought is, maybe he could live with you? Just until he got old enough to make it on his own."

She crammed all this in about a minute. Without waiting for my answer, she scribbled Joey's name and phone number on the back of an envelope that she had in her purse.

With that, she jumped up, "Here's my stop—glad there's somebody like you for kids like Joey. He used to be a great little kid—really. Will you talk to Joey?

I gave her my card and said I'd do what I could.

Loaded down with a couple of shopping bags filled with everything from bread to shoes, she made her way to the door and got off.

I breathed an audible sigh of relief and stared at Joey's name and address. I knew trying to help Joey would be difficult. We'd been through things like this before. We could count on little cooperation from his mom. The process would be long and complicated.

I wanted to toss his phone number away as easily as Joey's aunt had shoved the envelope into my hand. His mom had tossed away their responsibility for him. Instead, I slipped the envelope into my pocket, totally unsure about what, if anything, I could do for Joey.

I got off at the next stop and made my way through the crowd. The station was very busy, filled with determined people moving quickly, seemingly unaware of one another.

A kid in jeans and a once white T-shirt stood near the door. He had a beat-up knapsack which looked like it contained all of his belongings. He held up a sign he had made from a cardboard box.

"Will work for food," it read.

No one was paying any attention to him. He looked at each person, hoping to make eye contact with someone. But they all kept their eyes straight ahead or looked away. He was just one face in the crowd. No one wanted to acknowledge he was there.

I approached him and told him who I was. I asked if he'd like to come with me to the Home for supper.

"I won't promise you anything but a meal," I told him.

He told me he was new in town and needed work. He was nineteen and had been on the move since he was sixteen, traveling up and down the East and West coasts and many points between.

"I never had a permanent home since I was ten," he related, "and that was just a foster home. They decided they didn't want me either."

He refused my offer to help him find a permanent job.

"I better just keep moving for now," he said, "but I'll work for something to eat for tonight."

This kid would become just another face in the crowd of many kids that I had known over the years. They were in and out of my life as quickly as shooting stars. I would never know what became of any of them. After years of abuse and many homes, each found a set of wings that seemed to work. Each was afraid to trust anyone to help them find anything better.

I knew I couldn't help this kid, any more than I could help every kid I hear about who needs help. But he made me realize, and remember again, that I did help some of them. I couldn't give up.

I clenched my hand around the envelope in my pocket.

"Ok," I told him. "I have just one phone call to make when I get home."

Chapter Eighteen

PORTRAITS

Scattered through the halls and corridors of the Mercy Boys' Home are portraits of the kids who have made their home with us.

The staff and I are much like "old mother hens" when we show someone around. We like to stop and reminisce about a kid or an incident that was special to us. Those kids own part of our hearts.

On a particularly nostalgic day, sometimes it's hard for me to get anything done.

I guess, in this respect, those of us who work here share the feelings of most parents. Part of us is glad the boy or girl made it through the teen years successfully and is on his or her own. And part of us wants to recapture some of the moments we shared together along the way.

Kids new to the Home find these portraits interesting, too. There on the walls are the portraits of the boys and girls who have lived in our Home. It's proof to them we care.

Our kids, too, when they return, like to stroll the halls and remember other kids they knew during their time here.

They ask us, "What's Dave doing now?" or "Do you ever hear from Jason?"

And the fact that someone on our staff can usually tell them is what makes our kind of Home different from short-term shelters where kids usually come and go daily.

For better or worse, we stick with a kid over the long haul, much as most parents do with their kids.

Sometimes, in the heat of a discussion, one of our kids might yell, "Well, I didn't pick you for my parents." or "I don't really want to live here anymore."

And sometimes, after months of ups and downs with this particularly troubled kid, one of us might want to yell back, "And I wouldn't pick you for my kid." or "I wonder why we thought we could help you."

But what parent doesn't feel the same at some point in a child's growing up years?

The fact that parents and children do stay together, and keep loving and caring about one another through difficult times, is what separates "family" from acquaintances and even friends.

The intimate, unquestioned trust and security of family relationships is what we try to develop in our Mercy Home family, even though, at the end, we know our kids will leave us and may never return.

That's why, from the very beginning, our kids know, and we know, that their being here must be their choice.

It's risky for us. But it's also a big part of why I think out program has worked so well for over one hundred years. There's nothing magic to what we do. Basically, we do what any loving parent does. We use consistent discipline, values, and affection coupled with common sense.

We are an institution, yes. But we are also a family. And, like a family, we try to treat our kids as individuals in every way—even to the point of giving each a place of honor on our walls.

The individual portraits remind us, much more than a group shot ever could, of the uniqueness and worth of each of our kids.

As troubled teenagers, our kids come to us, each with a unique set of abilities, talents, and needs. As adults, our kids will leave us as mature, responsible persons.

Our responsibility is to see that when they do, they do so with two things — family roots to give them strength and love, and their own set of wings to take them onward. I wouldn't have it any other way.

EPILOGUE

I live at Mercy Boys' Home. I walk its halls, hear my footsteps echo in the stairwells, eat in the old school-like dining hall, and sleep there, just like the kids.

And let me tell you, it can be a frightening experience, living in this formidable old place.

In addition to kids' portraits, portraits of the Home's previous Superintendents hang on the walls. They are grouped together near the front entrance, not far from my office.

I have to pass them daily.

Like most old portraits of clergy, they look stern and very disciplined. Frozen in time, they seem to have all the virtues and all the answers that I don't.

Sometimes, after I've had a bad day or after I think I've bungled a situation with a kid, I feel guilty even walking past those esteemed figures.

I'd like to question them. What would you have done? Did you ever have to deal with the things I do? Were answers easier to come by when you were here?

I'd like to ask them all those things, and I'd like to get some firm answers.

Of course, even if I could communicate with them, they couldn't give me iron-clad answers. Kids are too individual to fit snugly into sealed containers and always have been.

And I know, too, from my own experience, that looking back on what has been is a lot easier than looking at what is, or what will be.

Yet, in reading through the records and notes of my predecessors and in reflecting upon my own childhood, I've come to the conclusion that, if things aren't more difficult for kids and parents today, they are definitely very different.

The world and the family have changed. One of the biggest changes is the lack of permanence—of everything.

I read recently that we are exposed to more information and experiences in one day than our ancestors were exposed to in their entire lifetimes.

That's got to be a jolt to anybody's system!

Everything was more clear-cut back in the old days, too. Parents didn't worry much about whether their way of raising kids was the best way. Usually their way was the only way that anyone knew. Churches, schools, governments, and other institutions operated in much the same way. There were right and wrong roads. A kid went down one of them or paid the consequences.

Today's "roads" are little more than dusty footpaths through dense forests and jungles. You often have to start walking, or running, without knowing either your destination or the problems you'll meet along the way.

All this ambiguity and "muddling through", as the great gurus like to refer to it, takes its toll. Most especially, I think, it impacts kids and their families.

By the year 2000, estimates are that 50 percent of America's families will be step-families. The majority of kids, at some point during their childhood years, will be raised by a single parent. Even more mothers than today's whopping 75 percent will be working outside the home.

Add those factors to the many other trends affecting society, and you have a situation nearly totally alien to what most of us knew when we were growing up.

No one theory, philosophy, social program, legislation, or source of funding is going to change these things. And, whether we have kids of our own or not, the problems of today's and tomorrow's families will affect all of us. They are already.

Nearly 25 percent of American kids drop out of high school. Many of the ones who do graduate have not learned the basic skills needed for employment. Jobs, more and more, demand advanced education, skills, and training. And I don't have to tell you that no one can raise a family with a minimum wage job—which is by far the most numerous and available job today.

Drugs and gangs permeate and even control areas in many of our cities. Crime and violence seem ever on the rise. And, through all of this, more and more pressure is exerted on the family.

Most of these families do not have the luxury of grandparents or other relatives living near them to share in their burdens. Isolated and alone, they must forge ahead and do the best they can.

Many can't. Many give up. And their kids suffer.

These are the kids I refer to as our *"new orphans"*

and our *"throwaway kids." In some ways, they are a reflection of our "quick-fix" attitude in general.*

What do we do with things we don't want? Throw them away! Our lives are touched daily with disposable products—from eating utensils and diapers, to razors and tools.

Use it once. Throw it away! If it doesn't work, or if it isn't perfect, pitch it and get a new one!

That, but in a more subtle, unspoken, and perhaps unconscious way, is the attitude of many parents about their kids, too. The trend is to have kids around when it's "convenient".

I knew two young doctors who postponed having a family until the birth of their child could be slid between their busy schedules and advanced training.

And, in spite of all this planning, the woman had the misfortune of becoming pregnant at an inappropriate time.

"You might know," she grumbled, "I'll be delivering right when I have to take my boards."

Then, too, there was a question of the baby's health. They intended to have an ultrasound test done. If there were any signs that the baby was anything less than perfect, they could take care of that with an abortion.

I have lost touch with this couple. But I often wonder how they and their child have fared. What happened when the child behaved badly, or embarrassed them in public, or was less than an A student in school? Did they have an answer for those things, too?

Poverty and many of the other factors which influence how a child fares in less affluent families was never a factor here. Yet the outcome was the same—the child had to be there when the parents wanted, and had to be what the parents wanted, or the child wouldn't be there at all.

Other parents may start out with more realistic expectations of what having a child means. They may be more accepting of their children initially. But when problems begin, or their family situation changes through unemployment, divorce, or ill health, they also look for ways to push their kids out the door. They drive them out the door, creating a new breed of orphan who is just as alone as any child whose parents have died.

Many of these are kids who are referred to Mercy Boys' Home and Mercy Girls' Home.

What's it like for these kids growing up with parents who don't want them?

What's it like for a fourteen year old kid to come home one night and have a parent say, "Get your stuff and get out—I've had enough!"?

What's it like to have a parent unemployed, stoned, drunk, abusive, and sick?

Personally, I don't know. What I do know I learned only through the eyes, minds, hearts, and souls of the kids at Mercy Boys' Home and Mercy Girls' Home.

They cry to me and sometimes lie to me. They love me and hate me. They ask me for things and sometimes give little in return. They exhilarate and disappoint me. In short, they do all the things I did to my parents, and all the things nearly all kids do to their parents sometimes.

But I hang in there with them anyway, just like my parents did for me.

No, they aren't really my biological kids. And no, we don't really have to take them in.

What they are is just kids. They need a place to live and someone to love them unconditionally. That's what Mercy Boys' Home and Mercy Girls' Home can give them and that's why we need to be here.

The Mission of Our Lady of Mercy
Mercy Boys' Home—Mercy Girls' Home

HOW IT ALL BEGAN

For Chicago's poor, the 1880s were far different from the "good old days" so romanticized in story and song.

Hundreds of young boys, the victims of family misfortunes, were thrown out on the streets to shift for themselves. They sold newspapers and shined shoes to earn a few pennies for food and bedded down for the night in open doorways, piano crates, or anywhere that afforded them some protection against the weather. Some of them were crippled or ill; few had much education—and all were unwanted and unloved.

But their plight did not go unnoticed.

In 1886, a group of priests met with the Most Reverend Patrick A. Feehan, the Archbishop of Chicago. Their conversation turned to Chicago's homeless children and how they could be helped.

Father Dennis Mahony, a Boston native who was working in the Chicago Archdiocese at the time, outlined a plan to alleviate the problem.

Archbishop Feehan became interested and assigned a diocesan priest, Father Louis Campbell, to open a home for the boys.

In 1887, Father Campbell rented several small

rooms above the Catholic library at La Salle and Madison Streets, and on November 3 of that year founded the Mission of Our Lady of Mercy, which over the years has come to be known as Mercy Boys' Home.

Shortly thereafter, Father rented a large, barn-like space at 45 E. Jackson Street, which soon became home to many of Chicago's troubled boys.

A kitchen stove was the main source of heat, making the place seem perpetually desolate and cold, particularly in the fall and winter months. On many nights, the boys bundled up in worn, donated clothing and crept into their painted iron beds to keep warm. For, although many generous people sent the orphans their cast-off clothing, few ever thought of sending bedding.

When Father Campbell's health failed, he was succeeded by Father Mahony, who was officially transferred to the Chicago Archdiocese.

A Shoestring Ministry

Father Mahony's work got off to a shaky financial start when his $200 a month rent was immediately increased to $300. Unable to pay the rent, Father was forced to close down the building. He scattered his boys among families and in cheap lodging houses while he sought additional funding and another location.

In 1889, he purchased a private residence at 1140 W. Jackson Boulevard, the present site of Mercy Boys' Home.

Father and the boys did their own cooking and tried to keep the house going in as dignified a manner as their scanty means permitted. Yet, the installments on the $24,000 loan on the house and other debts accumulated. During these lean years, only perseverance and an abiding faith in God kept the Home afloat.

Fortunately, as word of the Home's good work spread, many people contributed funds to help the homeless boys.

Poor health forced Father Mahony to retire.

Under the leadership of the new Superintendent, Fr. C.J. Quille, Mercy Boys' Home greatly expanded the scope of its ministry over the next 23 years.

Father realized that, to be most effective, he needed to provide the boys in his care with more than food, clothing, shelter and medical care. He purchased printing equipment to teach the boys a trade. He added a laundry, bathrooms, a recreation room, and a hall to accommodate the ever-growing number of boys.

Most importantly, however, Fr. Quille instituted ways to help the boys on a long-range basis by introducing educational and trade programs which would equip the boys with jobs skills.

With this expansion of programs and facilities, the Home was continually plagued with a lack of funds. Since it received no church or state monies, the Home depended solely on private contributions for its maintenance.

As Mercy Boys' Home continued to grow, larger facilities were needed. In 1910, a new red brick structure, large enough to accommodate 150 boys, was built at the site. This facility, which is still in use, increased the Home's debt to $70,000, a formidable sum for an institution with no fixed income. Despite these financial difficulties, Father was determined that the Home accept any boy who sought help.

As Mercy Boys' Home celebrated its 25th anniversary in 1912, Fr. Quille prophesied, "No matter what the passage of years may bring, the policy of the Mission (Mercy Boys' Home) shall remain invariably the same to the very end ... as it was formulated twenty-five years ago. It will receive and cherish and protect the child that needs its care."

Towards a Half Century of Caring

As the United States entered World War I, the finances and resources of Mercy Boys' Home were further strained. Forty boys left the Home to fight for their country.

To make ends meet, the Home began a new venture—mending shoes. In addition to helping conserve the country's resources, mending shoes provided much needed income. The Home's offer was one few could refuse.

"Mail your old shoes to us," their ads read. "We will repair them and return them to you with the bill. If you are satisfied, pay the bill. If you are not, tear up the bill. Your say-so goes with us. No strings to this offer. If there are, the strings are in your hands."

The success of the shoe-repair venture brought the Home into an era of expanded social action as well. Our boys volunteered their services for numerous community and charitable services.

As Mercy boys returned from the war, new efforts

were made to better equip them to enter the job market. The boys were further educated and taught trades such as printing, shoe repair, carpentry, auto mechanics, and retail and clerical skills.

More of the Home's efforts centered on rehabilitation. Athletic programs and extra curricular activities were established.

New Leadership

In 1929, as Father Quille left the Home to assume another ministry, his brother, Father A.G. Quille, succeeded him.

In 1933, Father Vincent W. Cooke was transferred from St. Mary's Training School to assume a one-year assignment at the Home. At the height of the Great Depression in 1934, Father Edward J. Kelly was named the Home's Superintendent.

Despite the poverty, homelessness, and unemployment plaguing the nation, Mercy Boys' Home continued to accept the many boys who came to its door. Once again, private donations kept the Home going during these difficult years.

As World War II began, the Mercy boys again rallied in support of their country. One hundred forty-eight of them served in World War II, six of those never to return.

Post War Years

The years after World War II can, in many ways, be considered some of the Home's most successful years. Father Kelly continued his work with homeless, unwanted, and troubled boys. By now, the boys were coming to the Home from towns and cities throughout the nation.

In both the Korean and the Vietnam Wars, boys from Mercy Boys' Home served in the Armed Forces, as they had during World War I and World War II.

Through its ongoing religious, educational, cultural, and social programs, the Home was successful in helping thousands of boys turn their lives around and become responsible citizens.

An Unexpected Turn of Events

In 1973, in his thirty-ninth year of service to Mercy Boys' Home, Father Kelly suffered a stroke. While he was recovering, he was diagnosed as having cancer.

Fr. James J. Close was sent from his parish duties to assist Fr. Kelly, now seriously ill. After Fr. Kelly's death that summer, Fr. Close was appointed the seventh Superintendent of the Home.

Under the leadership of Fr. Close, Mercy Boys' Home expanded its ministry to address the complex needs of troubled boys and girls of today. One of the greatest needs was to create an atmosphere which more closely duplicated a family and home setting.

Thus, Mercy Boys' Home was remodeled. The large one-room dorms were converted into smaller bedrooms for one or two boys.

In 1988, a home for teenage girls was opened in a private residence located in the Beverly-Morgan Park area of Chicago. Like Mercy Boys' Home, Mercy Girls' Home cares for teenagers from ages 14-18, although occasionally younger children are accepted in an effort to keep a family of brothers and sisters together.

The Family Unit—Always a Goal

Keeping the family unit together has long been one of our most important goals. Residential placement is always a last resort and is used only when the home and family situation are in crisis and no suitable foster home is available. When teenagers are referred to Mercy Boys' Home or Mercy Girls' Home, they literally have no where else to go and have no reliable adult capable of caring for them.

One or both of their parents may be living, and, in this sense, they are not the true "orphans" of years past. Yet, because of their desperate circumstances, they really are the *"new orphans,"* thrown on the streets because their parents and relatives are unable or refuse to take care of them.

Their educational and social problems are compounded. In addition, most have learning disabilities and emotional and behavior problems. Some have physical disabilities and medical problems as well. Some have experimented with drugs and alcohol. Some have had minor run-ins with the law. All require extensive counseling and professional help.

Referrals to Mercy Boys' Home and Mercy Girls' Home

About twenty percent of those accepted into our program are referred by the Courts and other social agencies.

The majority of the boys and girls come from private referrals. A concerned teacher, school counselor, pastor, parent, or relative may contact the home. Or a teenager will initiate his or her own referral. The parent or legal guardian usually is involved in the admission process. Every effort is made to retain these family ties once a placement is made.

Since Mercy Boys' Home and Mercy Girls' Home are designed for ongoing and extended care, a boy or girl can stay for a period of four or more years.

Admission is entirely voluntary—the teenager must want help and be willing to cooperate.

Before formal admission, for the child's benefit, the boy or girl is given an extensive battery of tests to determine intellectual, emotional, and psychological suitability.

Although an individual's program varies in structure according to his or her needs, each child must be enrolled in some type of educational program, and participate in the group sessions and activities at the Home. Most have part-time or full-time jobs.

Once a teenager is admitted, our Mercy program assumes complete responsibility for his or her care, and provides educational, medical, psychiatric, or psychological services as needed.

Our goal is to encourage the teenager to move towards greater independence and self-reliance. After age 18, Mercy Home residents receive follow-up and extended care through one of our several Aftercare programs, which are designed to help ease the transition from the Home to fully independent living.

Because of the unique design of our programs, the Mercy Boys' Home staff has greater leverage in deciding whom they will accept. Generally, we offer services to teenagers between the ages of 14 to 18, regardless of race, creed, or financial resources.

Those with serious drug or alcohol problems are referred to other facilities for treatment before admission.

PROGRAM EXPENSE

The cost of caring for a teenager at one of the Mercy Homes is obviously substantial. In cases where the parent or parents are able to contribute a portion of this amount, they are expected to do so.

Since nearly all of the teenagers in our Homes come from poor families unable to contribute little, if anything, toward the care of their children, Mercy Boys' Home and Mercy Girls' Home rely almost exclusively on private donations to fund its extensive ministry among troubled and homeless young people.

YOU CAN HELP!

The care of our boys and girls is only possible because of the financial support of friends who are interested in the future of these homeless kids.

Throughout our 103 years, our friends have judged that these kids are worth the effort. During our history, we've had some dark moments. In those crucial times, it was always friends who came to our aid. In a very practical way, they watch over us.

I have long called these special people our "angels".

They truly are the unseen guardians to our kids, helping us watch over them and show them the way to a better life.

"Guardian Angels" in the full sense of the word is what these wonderful, positive people have proved to be.

These are the people who understand the needs of our Home are ever ongoing and are willing to help in a regular, monthly way.

These people have established a continuous relationship with our kids from afar. The greatest joy they receive as our friend and supporter is the satisfaction of knowing they are insuring the future of homeless and abandoned girls and boys by providing them a safe place now.

If you would like more information, just call or visit us.

MERCY HOME FOR BOYS AND GIRLS
1140 West Jackson Boulevard
Chicago, Illinois 60607

(312) 738-7560

As a Guardian Angel, you will receive special remembrance in our prayers. And your name will be inscribed on a special Honor Roll in our chapel. . . in the hearts of the children in our Home.

SOME SOURCES OF HELP

National Center for Missing and Exploited Youth
(clearing house to help parents locate missing children)

(800) 643-5678

National Domestic Violence Hotline: Shelter Aid
(referrals for victims of domestic violence)

(800) 799-7233

National Institute on Drug Abuse Hotline
(crisis counseling for substance abusers)

(800) 662-4357

National Runaway Switchboard
(counseling and referrals for runaway youth and their families)

(800) 621-4000

The Runaway Hotline
(counseling and referrals for runaways)

(800) 231-6946

Please don't turn your back on homeless, abused and abandoned boys . . . they have no one else to turn to.

*"There are only two lasting bequests
we can give our children,
one is roots, the other wings."*

Mercy Home for Boys and Girls
1140 West Jackson Boulevard
Chicago, IL 60607-2906
(312) 738-7560